BLUE FUNNEL LINE

AN ILLUSTRATED HISTORY

Melampus in Birkenhead Docks. (C. McCutcheon)

BLUE FUNNEL LINE

AN ILLUSTRATED HISTORY

IAN COLLARD

AMBERLEY

Laertes (5) and *Lycaon* (3) berthed in the West Float at Birkenhead. (Malcolm Cranfield Collection)

First published 2010

Amberley Publishing Plc
Cirencester Road, Chalford,
Stroud, Gloucestershire, GL6 8PE

www.amberley-books.com

ISBN 978 1 84868 957 2

British Library Cataloguing in Publication Data.
A catalogue record for this book is available from the British Library.

Typesetting and Origination by FONTHILLDESIGN.
Printed in Great Britain.

CONTENTS

ACKNOWLEDGEMENTS

I would like to thank the following people for all the help and assistance they have given me in the preparation of this book: Dave Molyeneux of the Blue Funnel Association; Victor Young of Wellington, New Zealand; Captain Glynne Pritchard; Justin Merrigan; Alan Lee; John and Marion Clarkson; H. M. Le Fleming; Barry Shore; and the wealth of information kindly provided by Duncan Haws.

INTRODUCTION

I was born and brought up less than half a mile from where the Blue Funnel Line ships berthed at Vittoria Dock, Birkenhead. The company loaded cargo in three berths at Vittoria Dock and at another in the East Float, and there was always a Blue Funnel to be seen in Birkenhead Docks or on the Mersey.

The company was formed by the visionary Alfred Holt, who was convinced that the steamship would provide a better and more economical way of shipping cargo and passengers to the Far East, China and later to Australia. He purchased the three-masted sailing ship *Dumbarton Youth* and fitted her with two direct-action engines.

Alfred and his younger brother Philip embarked on a great adventure and decided to give their ships names from Greek mythology, starting with *Agamemnon*, *Ajax* and *Achilles*. The Ocean Steamship Company was founded in 1865, and over the following years, various feeder services and storage facilities were developed at the main trading ports. By 1900, the line owned forty-one ships with a gross tonnage of 165,646 tons.

A limited company was formed in 1902, and the China Mutual Steam Navigation was acquired. The Indra Line and Knight Line were taken over, and between 1919 and 1934, forty-eight new ships were constructed for the company. A joint service was arranged with the Aberdeen White Star Line, and with the large demand for passenger accommodation in the Far East trades, new vessels with extensive passenger accommodation were introduced. In 1935, the Glen Line and its services were purchased and a controlling interest in the Straits Steamship Company was acquired.

Forty-one ships were lost during the Second World War and a rebuilding programme was started with the launching of the *Anchises*-class vessel, *Calchas*, by Mrs Lawrence Holt in 1946. Twenty-one similar vessels were introduced over the next seven years and Lawrence Holt retired in 1953. Elder Dempster Lines was taken over in 1965, and the company became Ocean Fleets Limited two years later.

William Cory & Son Limited was acquired in the early 1970s, when the shipping industry was being forced to come to terms with the transformation of freight in containers. Shipping operators amalgamated and joint services were developed with new ships and technology. Overseas Containers Limited was formed, and the company diversified with the building of bulk carriers and tankers. Another change followed in 1967, when the name Alfred Holt disappeared, with the company becoming Ocean Transport & Trading in 1972.

The company moved out of deep-sea trading in 1989, and the towage interests were sold in 2000. Ocean Group and the National Freight Corporation merged that year, forming Exel plc, and Deutsche Post took over Exel in 2005.

The loading berths at Vittoria Dock have been empty for many years, as the container trade has moved across the river to the Royal Seaforth Dock. The port operator, Peel Holdings, has announced plans for a major development to transform Birkenhead Docks into Wirral Waters. This will involve the development of more than 500 acres of the dock estate to build retail and leisure facilities, hotels, shops, bars, restaurants, with the East Float and Vittoria Dock becoming the central sector of this project. This will include buildings of over fifty storeys, pedestrian bridges will link all parts of this area, and the waterside setting will enhance the retail, commercial and residential developments. Perhaps the maritime legacy of Alfred Holt will be remembered in this development, together with the other shipping lines that provided employment and services from the Mersey to ports around the world.

Ian Collard
Wallasey, April 2010

THE BLUE FUNNEL LINE
Alfred Holt & Co Liverpool
TO THE FAR EAST SOUTH AFRICA AUSTRALIA & INDONESIA
WALTER THOMAS
FAST CARGO & PASSENGER SERVICES

THE BLUE FUNNEL LINE
TO
THE FAR EAST
INDONESIA
AUSTRALIA
&
SOUTH AFRICA
(PASSENGERS ONLY)
ALFRED HOLT & Co
LIVERPOOL
FAST FREIGHT & PASSENGER SERVICES

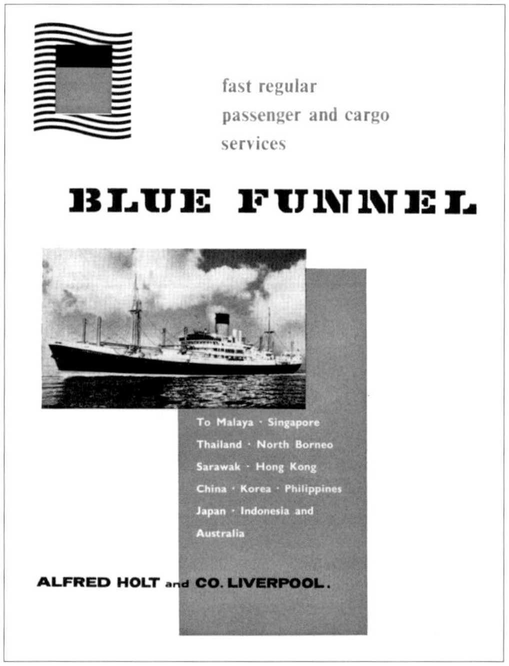
fast regular
passenger and cargo
services
BLUE FUNNEL
To Malaya · Singapore
Thailand · North Borneo
Sarawak · Hong Kong
China · Korea · Philippines
Japan · Indonesia and
Australia
ALFRED HOLT and CO. LIVERPOOL.

THE BLUE FUNNEL LINE

Alfred Holt was born in 1829, and was the son of George Holt, who was a Liverpool businessman involved in cotton, banking and insurance. In 1836, George Holt helped to found the Liverpool Fire & Life Assurance Company, which helped to establish Liverpool as a cotton insurance centre. Alfred was apprenticed to Edward Woods, the railway engineer for the Liverpool & Manchester Railway, and was employed by the London & North Western Railway when it was formed in 1846. He completed his apprenticeship in 1850 and specialised in boiler design. However, the slump in railway development at this time meant that he had to seek other work, and in 1851, he was working in the shipping company Lamport & Holt, which had been formed by his older brother George and William James Lamport. He became their shipping consultant, dealing with shipowning, planning, management and contractual work. Later, in 1851, Alfred sailed to Sicily, Egypt and Syria as an engineer in the *Orontes* on her maiden voyage.

The following year, he established himself as a consulting engineer and initially worked with Edward Woods on trials and bollard pull calculations for locomotives, and in 1852, Alfred Holt was involved in managing the *Alpha* and the William Denny-built *Dumbarton Youth*, a three-masted sailing ship which was owned by Thomas Ainsworth and Alfred's father, George Holt. She was fitted with two direct-action engines, and as he was a railway engineer, he was able to replace the engines with those of his own design. Following the success of the project, he persuaded his father and Thomas Ainsworth to order a second ship for the mineral and coal trade, which was named *Cleator* and was built by Cato & Miller at Brunswick Dock, Liverpool, in 1854. She was chartered to the French Government during the Crimean War for the rate of *62s 6d* per registered ton per month and he was then able to construct a larger vessel, which he named *Saladin*, which was placed on the West Indian trade.

She was followed by the *Plantagenet*, *Talisman*, *Askalon* and *Crusader*, which were built at very competitive rates because of a depression in the shipbuilding industry in 1857. Alfred's father, George Holt, died in 1861, and he was joined by his younger brother Philip. By 1864, increased competition affected the profits of the operation, and he sold all of his ships, apart from the *Cleator*, to the West India & Pacific Steamship Company.

He soon began to look at the prospects of operating a service to the Far East, and *Cleator* was re-engined with single-crank tandem-compound machinery that had been designed by Alfred. The engine was designed to inject steam into a high-pressure cylinder and then a low-pressure cylinder, which were placed in tandem and operated a single balanced crankshaft with a flywheel counterweight, which cut coal consumption by 40 per cent and increased the speed by 2 knots. She completed a series of successful trials late in 1864 commanded by Captain Isaac Middleton. *Cleator* operated to France and then two voyages to Brazil. The Ocean Steamship Company was formed on 11 January 1865, and an order worth £156,000 was placed with Scott's of Greenock for *Agamemnon*, *Ajax* and *Achilles*. The three ships were designed as square-rigged barques of 2,280 tons and were funded by the earlier sale of the five ships, and from loans from other members of the family and local businessmen.

On 19 April 1866, the first of these, *Agamemnon*, sailed from Liverpool to the Far East under the command of Captain Middleton, calling at Penang, Singapore, Hong Kong and Shanghai. She was followed by *Ajax* on 30 June and *Achilles*. The three vessels were 2,280 tons, 310 feet in length by 39 feet beam and had a service speed of 10 knots. These vessels proved to be very economical to operate, and *Achilles* took fifty-seven days and eighteen hours to return home from China via the Cape on her voyage of 12,532 miles. She carried 2,800 tons of cargo and consumed less than 20 tons of coal a day.

Above left *Glaucus* in the Suez Canal.

Above right: *Antenor*.

Left: *Deucalion* leads a convoy in the Suez Canal.

Diomed and *Nestor*, of 1,850 tons, were delivered in 1868. On 16 September 1868, the steamer *Ajax* sank at Shanghai following temporary repairs to the propeller shaft by the engineer. The accident was caused by design fault and future ships were fitted with a watertight gland in the propeller shaft. *Diomed* was the first of the line's vessels to pass through the Suez Canal, in March 1870. The voyage through the Suez Canal was 3,300 miles shorter, saving ten to twelve days.

In 1869, *Cleator* sailed to China, Melbourne in Australia, and then to Singapore. *Cleator* was sold to Captain John D. Ross of Singapore in 1872, renamed *Alastor*, spending the next twenty years trading to Labuan. *Priam* and *Sarpedon* were introduced in 1870, *Hector*, *Ulysses*, *Menelaus* and *Glaucus* in 1871, *Patroclus*, *Deucalion* and *Antenor* in 1872. Sailings from London were operated briefly in 1880, and by 1883, it became a port of discharge only when a regular weekly service operated from the Port of Liverpool to China and later Japan. The company's interests were looked after by Butterfield and Swire in China and Japan, and Mansfield, Bogaardt & Company in Singapore. An important element of the success of the company was the choice of agents in the Far East and the decision to allow them to be shareholders. This gave them a stake in the company and the motivation to increase business and profits. In 1872, John Swire formed the China Navigation Company to provide local shipping services in China.

Alfred Holt had at his disposal two private yachts in which he took summer holidays. The first *Argo* was built by Scott & Company at Greenock in 1875, but was sold after five years in service. The second *Argo* was also built by Scott's in 1885 and took Alfred Holt and his family on holidays to Iceland, Jamaica and Constantinople. In 1893, she left Liverpool Landing Stage on 19 June under the command of Captain H. Johnsen for a cruise to the Norwegian Fjords calling at Oban and Bergen, where Mrs Holt joined the ship. The ship sailed to Stavanger and into several of the fjords, including the Hardanger Fjord and the Sorfjord. They returned via the Faroe Islands and proceeded to Port Erin on the Isle of Man, where they anchored for a couple of days, arriving back at Liverpool on 9 August.

The two-funnelled vessels *Stentor*, *Orestes* and *Anchises* were delivered in 1875 and *Hector* struck a reef and sank in October that year and was one of a number of collisions, breakdowns and groundings that took place at this time in the development of the fleet. *Orestes* sank off Galle in March 1876 and *Sarpedon* was lost following a collision off Ushant in September that year. Consequently, the Holt brothers decided that they would not insure their ships and would assume the whole of the risk of the vessels. Following the reduction in the price of tea, shipping rates fell and *Antenor* was chartered to Lamport & Holt for their South American services. Intense competition was driving freight rates and profits down on the Far Eastern routes, which led to the establishment of the Conference Agreement in 1879, whereas stable freight rates could be offered by the various shipping lines in the service. In theory, the conference was to help regulate competition and stabilise freight rates and passenger fares, but some members undercut rates to attract business from the other lines. The members of the conference were Blue Funnel Line, Glen Line, Castle Line, Peninsular & Oriental Line and the French company Messageries Maritimes.

Ganymede was introduced to operate from Belawan Deli, Sumatra, to Singapore with tobacco in 1880, and *Jason*, *Laertes*, *Cyclops*, *Bellerophon* and *Telemachus* were delivered. John Swire resigned as Chairman of the Far Eastern Shipping Conference in 1882.

The vessels' loading berth on the Mersey was transferred to Birkenhead from Liverpool in 1883, when services were offered to Gibraltar, Malta, Aden, Colombo, Amoy and Nagasaki. The storage hulk *Sarah Nicholson* was moored at Belewan Deli followed by *Ascanius*, and the *Andes* was placed at Penang. These were followed by *Mercury* in 1881, *Hebe* in 1885, and *Calypso* in 1885. One of the major trades was tobacco, and these were used for storage prior to shipment to Europe. *Hecuba* was placed on the Bangkok to Singapore rice trade, and she was followed by *Hecate* in 1885, *Medusa* in 1886 and *Hydra* in 1889. *Telamon*, *Titan* and *Palamed* entered service in 1885, and *Teucer* was lost off Ushant. *Palinurus*, *Prometheus* and *Dardanus* were introduced the following year. The line started to operate a service from Glasgow on 16 February 1887. *Memnon* and *Ranee* were bought for the Singapore to North Borneo service, and this trade was extended to Manado, Ternate and the Moluccas by *Banjermassin*, *Devonhurst*, *Flintshire*, *Kongsee* and *Normanby*. On establishment of the Straits Steamship Company in 1890, *Sappho* and *Will o' the Wisp* were transferred to the line.

To compete with the Dutch shipping lines, Nederlandsche Stoomvaart Maatschappij 'Oceaan' was formed in Amsterdam in 1891, and the East India Ocean Steamship Company was established to operate from Singapore but was sold to North German Lloyd the following year. The changing pattern of trade on the routes led to a new conference system, and new vessels were built which were better suited for the carriage of the new cargoes, and the Homeward Conference was joined by the China Mutual Steam Navigation Company in 1891.

Captain Frank Pitts was sent to Australia by Alfred Holt in 1889 to 'look at the prospects and report on the possibilities of running a service from Fremantle up the coast of Western Australia via Java to Singapore'. The *Saladin* and *Sultan* were built in 1890 for this service, and an agreement was made with the West Australian Steamship Company to run a joint fortnightly service on this route.

Left and above: India Buildings, Liverpool.

Tydeus in Alfred Dock, Birkenhead.

A Blue Funnel vessel transits the Suez Canal.

Protesilaus.

Titan (2) in the Mersey.

Ixion, *Tantalus*, *Ulysses* and *Pyrrhus*, which were delivered in 1892, were designed as three-island-type vessels with a large funnel and were the predecessors of the distinctive design. Mr H. B. Wortley joined the company as the naval architect in 1893 and was responsible for the design of many of the ships and was later made a director of the line. The new *Orestes*, *Sarpedon*, *Diomed*, *Hector*, *Menelaus* and *Dardanus*, together with the *Nestor* (ex-*Queen of India*), joined the fleet in 1894-95, and seven ships were sold to Japan. A service from Manchester was offered during 1895-96, but this proved to be unsuccessful.

Richard Durning Holt, who later became a Liberal Member of Parliament, Maurice Llewelyn Davies and George Holt Junior joined the company in 1895, and Albert Crompton had become manager in 1882. They embarked on a reorganisation and rationalisation of the line, resulting in a 15 per cent reduction in salaries and wages. In addition, the decline in the price of coal and the reduction in the Suez Canal dues resulted in a net profit of £27,500 in 1892 and £266,100 in 1902. *Antenor*, *Glaucus*, *Patroclus* and *Prometheus* were introduced in 1896 and the triple-expansion-engined *Ulysses* was delivered two years later. The company bought the West Australian Steam Navigation Company's half share in the *Sultan* in 1898, following the line's purchase of the *Karrakatta*. This gave each company two vessels each on the Singapore to Fremantle route. The East India Company was sold to Norddeutscher Lloyd in 1899, and between 1894 and 1902, twenty-two new Blue Funnel ships were added to the fleet.

A cargo service to Australia commenced in 1901 with vessels loading at Glasgow and later at Liverpool, following the establishment of a service from Fremantle to Java and Singapore, which began operating in 1890. Expansion followed the increase in world trade with tin and rubber from the Malay states, tobacco from the East Indies, and fruit and meat from Australia, with British manufactured goods shipped on the outward voyages.

The Ocean Steamship Company became a limited company in 1902. In 1910, *Aeneas*, *Ascanius* and *Anchises* enabled the company to provide a passenger service on this route, calling at South Africa on the way to Australia. *Sarpedon*, *Nestor* and *Orestes* were fitted with refrigeration holds for the carriage of perishable cargoes. *Nestor* and *Ulysses* followed in 1913 carrying meat, apples, timber and sugar, and refrigerated cargoes such as meat and butter on the inward voyages. A loss of £5,700 in 1905 was turned into a profit of £91,600 in 1913 on the Australian services. *Nestor* made her last voyage in 1950 after giving the company thirty-eight years service in peace and two world wars.

In 1902, the China Mutual Steam Navigation Company was taken over with its fleet of thirteen relatively modern vessels. These were the *Oopack*, *Ching Wo* (b.1894), *Kaisow*, *Pak Ling*, *Kintuck*, *Moyune*, *Teenkai* (b.1895), *Yang Tsze*, *Ping Suey*, *Hyson* (b.1899) and *Keemun*, *Ningchow*, *Oanfa* (b.1902-03). The line had been in operation since 1882 and traded from China to parts of Canada and the United States. It started sailings between the Straits Settlements, Java and the Pacific Coast of America, and later from China, Japan and the West Coast of America. Ocean Building was opened in Singapore in 1903 and Mansfield's were incorporated as a limited company. Between 1903 and 1905, eight new ships were ordered and another six between 1908 and 1910.

Alfred Holt resigned as manager of the line in 1904. His brother Philip had resigned in 1897, followed by Albert Crompton in 1901, and William Stapledon was appointed manager in 1902. Land was purchased at Kowloon and Shanghai in 1905 and wharfs and warehouses were constructed, and later, similar resources were constructed at Hankow, Batavia, Surabaya and Macassar. Henry Bell Wortley and Lawrence Durning Holt were appointed as managers in 1908, and George Holt retired because of ill health and was replaced by Charles Sydney in 1912.

The *Bellerophon*, *Teucer*, *Antilochus*, *Cyclops* and *Titan* of 1906 were most distinctive, as they were designed with twin masts or goal posts designed to enable derricks to work at the maximum outboard radius. Consequently, the *Bellerophon* class were nicknamed the 'football ships'. Two of these ships were lost in the Second World War, but the remaining three survived until 1948 when they were forty-two years old. *Ixion* was a total loss following a fire in 1911, and *Perseus* and *Theseus* joined the fleet in 1908, followed by *Neleus*, *Atreus* and *Rhesus* in 1911, *Demodocus* and *Laomedon* in 1912, *Eumaeus* and *Phemius* in 1913, *Protesilaus* in 1910 and *Talthybius* and *Ixion* in 1912 for the trans-Pacific service.

Opposite: Patroclus (2) aground at Portland Bill in September, 1907.

Right: Nestor (3).

Above: Anchises (3) at Hobart, Tasmania, in November 1939.

Left: Evan R. Pritchard, Chief Officer of the *Talthybius* in 1930, was with Blue Funnel from 1918, as third mate of the *Menelaus*, to 1931, when he left the company as mate of the *Eurylochus* to join British Rail at Holyhead. He was born on 6 August 1892 and was one of seven children born to Capt. Richard Pritchard and his wife Ellen. Richard was master on Trinity House light vessels.

Evan joined his first ship, the sailing ship *Royal*, on 30 November 1909, signing on as Mess Room Steward at Barry for a voyage to the River Plate. His final voyage in sail was on the *Gwydyr Castle*, which took him around the world on a voyage lasting from 14 April 1913 to 23 October 1914. The famous marine artist Anton Otto Fischer was on this ship some years previously and his experiences and paintings are recorded in the book *Foc'sle Days*. Evan R. Pritchard held a 'Square Rig' Master's ticket and joined Lamport & Holt's, and whilst Third Officer of *Tennyson*, he and the Radio Officer were commissioned by the Admiralty to charter a fishing boat with local crew to search the islands of the Amazon basin for evidence of the German raider *Moewe*. Also during that voyage, an attempt was made to blow the ship up with a bomb planted in New York by members of the Duquesne spy ring. Three seamen were killed by the explosion, and the ship was extensively damaged.

Evan was married with a young son by this time and wanted to be closer to home. To this end, he joined LMS Steamers at Holyhead. He was Chief Officer of the *Scotia* when she was bombed at Dunkirk, and later on *Cambria* when she was strafed by a German aircraft in the Irish Sea, when the Third Officer died of a bullet wound to the thigh. He died at home on 2 Feb 1951 after a short illness, aged fifty-eight.

His son, Idwal, was AB with the company, gaining second mate before moving on to Lamport & Holt's and Clan line before also moving on to the Ferries at Holyhead, retiring as Senior Master of the *St David*. His other son, Glynne, joined the company in 1956 as midshipman and left in 1968 as second mate of the *Dolius*, to join British Rail at Holyhead. His wife accompanied him on his final voyage, and he retired through ill health as Master of *St Cybi* in 1991.

Above left: *Antenor* (2).

Above right: *Diomed* (4).

Right: *Ulysses* (4) passing under the almost-completed Sydney Harbour Bridge.

Nestor and *Ulysses*, of 14,500 gross tons, became the largest vessels in the fleet when they were delivered in 1913. They were twin-screw with a speed of 14 ½ knots and had accommodation for 280 passengers. *Lycaon* and *Helenus* were delivered in 1913 and *Troilus*, *Agapenor*, *Mentor*, *Teiresias* and *Pyrrhus* in 1914. *Troilus* was the company's first war loss and was replaced by a new vessel of the same name in 1916. *Elpenor* and *Diomed* were delivered the following year and *Tyndareus*, a larger 'football ship' was delivered in 1916.

Alfred Holt died on 28 November 1911 and his brother Philip on 27 November 1914. The opening of the Panama Canal in 1914 enabled the company to provide a service from the United Kingdom to the West Coast of America and *Astyanax* was the first Blue Funnel vessel to use the canal, in February 1915. At the beginning of the First World War, the Blue Funnel Line owned sixty-nine ships, and during hostilities, the company lost eighteen ships and had twenty-nine others damaged by shellfire, torpedoes or mines. The Indra Line was purchased in 1915, enabling the line to provide a regular service between New York and the Far East, and the ships were given Blue Funnel names:

Indrasamba	was renamed	*Eurydamas*
Indrawadi	"	*Eurymedon*
Inverclyde	"	*Eurymachus*
Indradeo	"	*Eurybates*
Indraghiri	"	*Eurylochus*
Indrakuala	"	*Eurypylus*
Indra	"	*Euryades*

The Midshipmen's Department was established in 1916 as a training facility for deck officers. The programme included training in seamanship, navigational duties and cargo operations in port. A hostel was opened in Liverpool and midshipmen were assessed on a regular basis.

In 1917, the Knight Line was acquired with the four ships of their fleet, *Knight of the Garter*, *Knight of the Thistle*, *Knight Templar* and *Knight Companion*. Alfred Holt purchased the line for £60,000 and the Knight Line was wound up showing a profit of £428,666 8*s* 5*d*. *Knight of the Garter* and *Knight of the Thistle* were registered as owned by the China Mutual Steam Navigation Company and *Knight Templar* and *Knight Companion* went to the Ocean Steamship Company. *Knight of the Thistle* foundered on 10 December 1917 on a voyage from New York to London. The crew of sixty-four were rescued by the *Vulcan* and taken to Boston.

The following vessels were lost during the First World War:

Troilus	19.10.14	Cruiser Emden in the Indian Ocean
Diomed (2)	22.08.15	U-38 off Queenstown, Ireland
Achilles	31.03.16	U-boat in Atlantic
Perseus	21.02.17	Mined off Colombo
Troilus (2)	2.05.17	U-boat in Atlantic
Calchas	11.05.17	U-boat off Ireland
Phemius	4.06.17	U-boat off Northern Ireland
Laertes	1.08.17	U-boat off Devon
Kintuck	2.12.17	Mined off St Ives, Cornwall
Eumaeus	26.02 18	U-boat in English Channel
Machaon	27.02.18	U-boat in Mediterranean
Autolycus	12.04.18	U-boat off Cape Palos
Moyune	12.04.18	U-boat off Cape Palos
Glaucus	3.06.18	U-boat in Mediterranean
Diomed (3)	21.08.18	U-boat in Atlantic
Oopack	4.10.18	U-boat in Mediterranean

The *Veghtstroom* and *Elve*, which were also owned by the company, were lost in 1917. On 6 February 1917, *Tyndareus* was mined off Cape Agulhas with members of the 25th Bn Middlesex Regiment on board, who were successfully transferred to *Oxfordshire* and *Eumaeus*. *Tyndareus* was turned around and her crew sailed her to Simonstown to be repaired. Over 132,000 British and Commonwealth and 116,000 American troops were carried on Blue Funnel vessels as well as Portuguese soldiers and Chinese labourers.

Aeneas.

Philoctetes entering Alfred lock at Birkenhead.

At the end of the war, the company had lost eighteen ships and several ships were fitted with temporary passenger accommodation at the request of the British Government. The Eastern Shipping Company Limited was purchased in 1922 together with its shipyard at Penang. The steam turbine vessels *Sarpedon*, *Patroclus*, *Hector* and *Antenor* were introduced from 1923 and were the company's first ships with substantial passenger accommodation, and the first diesel-engine vessel, *Medon*, joined the fleet in 1923 followed by *Tantalus*. On 4 March 1924, *Ascanius* took the first sailing on a new joint service with the White Star Line to Australian ports, which was joined by the Aberdeen Line two years later. The line moved its operations to the new India Buildings at Liverpool in 1928. Following the collapse of the Royal Mail Group, Richard Holt was appointed as Chairman of Elder Dempster Lines. For most of the period between the world wars, trade was well below its 1913 level and declined even further during the Great Depression, from 1928 to 1933.

From 1919 to 1934, the company ordered twenty-eight new vessels, and in 1935, they acquired the London-based Glen Line, which retained its own red funnel and traditional 'glen' names. Glen Line was founded in 1869 as Alan C. Gow & Company, became McGregor, Gow & Company in 1880, and joined with the Shire Line in 1911. Orders were placed for eight motorships by the Glen Line in 1936, three were delivered at the outbreak of the war, and when the other vessels of the class were completed, they were all requisitioned by the Admiralty.

In 1936, the Ocean Steamship Company purchased 675,000 shares in Elder Dempster Lines Holdings Ltd, becoming the largest shareholder and taking control of the company.

The origins of the line can be traced back to the 1830s, but it was not until 1868 that Elder Dempster & Company was appointed as the agency to run a shipping service from Glasgow and Liverpool to West Africa. Alfred Jones was given a junior partnership in Elder Dempster Line in 1879, and by 1884, he controlled the company. On his death, the line was acquired by Sir Owen Cosby Phillips and Lord Pirrie, forming Elder Dempster & Company Limited.

Above: The cover of the Blue Funnel travel brochure 'Opportunities for Travel 1934-35'.

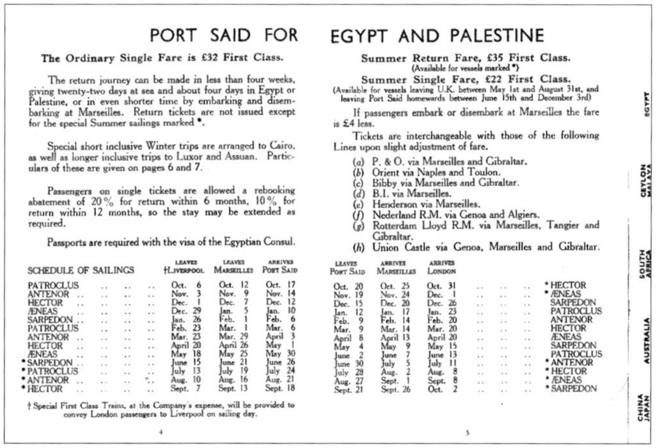

PORT SAID FOR EGYPT AND PALESTINE

The Ordinary Single Fare is £32 First Class.

The return journey can be made in less than four weeks, giving twenty-two days at sea and about four days in Egypt or Palestine, or in even shorter time by embarking and disembarking at Marseilles. Return tickets are not issued except for the special Summer sailings marked *.

Special short inclusive Winter trips are arranged to Cairo, as well as longer inclusive trips to Luxor and Assuan. Particulars of these are given on pages 6 and 7.

Passengers on single tickets are allowed a rebooking abatement of 20% for return within 6 months, 10% for return within 12 months, so the stay may be extended as required.

Passports are required with the visa of the Egyptian Consul.

Summer Return Fare, £35 First Class.
(Available for vessels marked *)

Summer Single Fare, £22 First Class.
(Available for vessels leaving U.K. between May 1st and August 31st, and leaving Port Said homewards between June 15th and December 3rd)

If passengers embark or disembark at Marseilles the fare is £4 less.

Tickets are interchangeable with those of the following Lines upon slight adjustment of fare.

(*a*) P. & O. via Marseilles and Gibraltar.
(*b*) Orient via Naples and Toulon.
(*c*) Bibby via Marseilles and Gibraltar.
(*d*) B.I. via Marseilles.
(*e*) Henderson via Marseilles.
(*f*) Nederland R.M. via Genoa and Algiers.
(*g*) Rotterdam Lloyd R.M. via Marseilles, Tangier and Gibraltar.
(*h*) Union Castle via Genoa, Marseilles and Gibraltar.

SCHEDULE OF SAILINGS	Leaves †Liverpool	Leaves Marseilles	Arrives Port Said	Leaves Port Said	Arrives Marseilles	Arrives London	
PATROCLUS	Oct. 6	Oct. 12	Oct. 17	Oct. 20	Oct. 25	Oct. 31	* HECTOR
ANTENOR	Nov. 3	Nov. 9	Nov. 14	Nov. 19	Nov. 24	Dec. 1	* ÆNEAS
HECTOR	Dec. 1	Dec. 7	Dec. 12	Dec. 15	Dec. 20	Dec. 26	SARPEDON
ÆNEAS	Dec. 29	Jan. 5	Jan. 10	Jan. 12	Jan. 17	Jan. 23	PATROCLUS
SARPEDON	Jan. 26	Feb. 1	Feb. 6	Feb. 9	Feb. 14	Feb. 20	ANTENOR
PATROCLUS	Feb. 23	Mar. 1	Mar. 6	Mar. 9	Mar. 14	Mar. 20	HECTOR
ANTENOR	Mar. 23	Mar. 29	April 3	April 8	April 13	April 20	ÆNEAS
HECTOR	April 20	April 26	May 1	May 4	May 9	May 15	SARPEDON
ÆNEAS	May 18	May 25	May 30	June 2	June 7	June 13	PATROCLUS
* SARPEDON	June 15	June 21	June 26	June 30	July 5	July 11	* ANTENOR
* PATROCLUS	July 13	July 19	July 24	July 28	Aug. 2	Aug. 8	* HECTOR
* ANTENOR	Aug. 10	Aug. 16	Aug. 21	Aug. 27	Sept. 1	Sept. 8	* ÆNEAS
* HECTOR	Sept. 7	Sept. 13	Sept. 18	Sept. 21	Sept. 26	Oct. 2	* SARPEDON

† Special First Class Trains, at the Company's expense, will be provided to convey London passengers to Liverpool on sailing day.

4 5

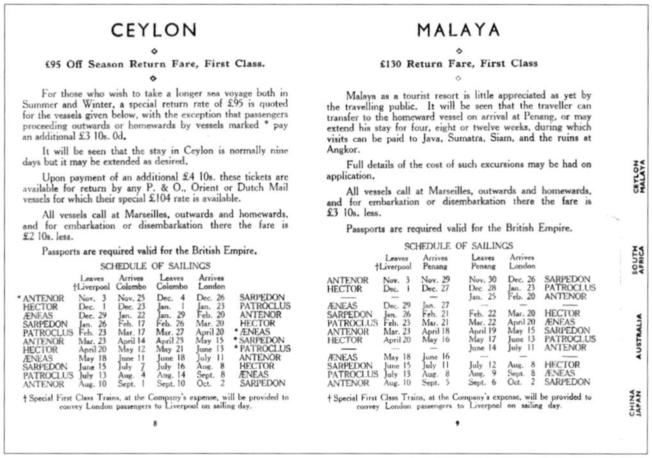

CEYLON

£95 Off Season Return Fare, First Class.

For those who wish to take a longer sea voyage both in Summer and Winter, a special return rate of £95 is quoted for the vessels given below, with the exception that passengers proceeding outwards or homewards by vessels marked * pay an additional £3 10s. 0d.

It will be seen that the stay in Ceylon is normally nine days but it may be extended as desired.

Upon payment of an additional £4 10s. these tickets are available for return by any P. & O., Orient or Dutch Mail vessels for which their special £104 rate is available.

All vessels call at Marseilles, outwards and homewards, and for embarkation or disembarkation there the fare is £2 10s. less.

Passports are required valid for the British Empire.

SCHEDULE OF SAILINGS

	Leaves †Liverpool	Arrives Colombo	Leaves Colombo	Arrives London	
* ANTENOR	Nov. 3	Nov. 25	Dec. 4	Dec. 26	SARPEDON
HECTOR	Dec. 1	Dec. 23	Jan. 1	Jan. 23	PATROCLUS
ÆNEAS	Dec. 29	Jan. 22	Jan. 29	Feb. 20	ANTENOR
SARPEDON	Jan. 26	Feb. 17	Feb. 26	Mar. 20	HECTOR
PATROCLUS	Feb. 23	Mar. 17	Mar. 27	April 20	* ÆNEAS
ANTENOR	Mar. 23	April 14	April 23	May 15	* SARPEDON
HECTOR	April 20	May 12	May 21	June 13	* PATROCLUS
ÆNEAS	May 18	June 11	June 18	July 11	ANTENOR
SARPEDON	June 15	July 7	July 16	Aug. 8	HECTOR
PATROCLUS	July 13	Aug. 4	Aug. 14	Sept. 8	ÆNEAS
ANTENOR	Aug. 10	Sept. 1	Sept. 10	Oct. 2	SARPEDON

† Special First Class Trains, at the Company's expense, will be provided to convey London passengers to Liverpool on sailing day.

8

MALAYA

£130 Return Fare, First Class

Malaya as a tourist resort is little appreciated as yet by the travelling public. It will be seen that the traveller can transfer to the homeward vessel on arrival at Penang, or may extend his stay for four, eight or twelve weeks, during which visits can be paid to Java, Sumatra, Siam, and the ruins at Angkor.

Full details of the cost of such excursions may be had on application.

All vessels call at Marseilles, outwards and homewards, and for embarkation or disembarkation there the fare is £3 10s. less.

Passports are required valid for the British Empire.

SCHEDULE OF SAILINGS

	Leaves †Liverpool	Arrives Penang	Leaves Penang	Arrives London	
ANTENOR	Nov. 3	Nov. 29	Nov. 30	Dec. 26	SARPEDON
HECTOR	Dec. 1	Dec. 27	Dec. 28	Jan. 23	PATROCLUS
—	—	—	Jan. 25	Feb. 20	ANTENOR
ÆNEAS	Dec. 29	Jan. 27	—	—	—
SARPEDON	Jan. 26	Feb. 21	Feb. 22	Mar. 20	HECTOR
PATROCLUS	Feb. 23	Mar. 21	Mar. 22	April 20	ÆNEAS
ANTENOR	Mar. 23	April 18	April 19	May 15	SARPEDON
HECTOR	April 20	May 16	May 17	June 13	PATROCLUS
—	—	—	June 14	July 11	ANTENOR
ÆNEAS	May 18	June 16	—	—	—
SARPEDON	June 15	July 11	July 12	Aug. 8	HECTOR
PATROCLUS	July 13	Aug. 8	Aug. 9	Sept. 8	ÆNEAS
ANTENOR	Aug. 10	Sept. 5	Sept. 6	Oct. 2	SARPEDON

† Special First Class Trains, at the Company's expense, will be provided to convey London passengers to Liverpool on sailing day.

9

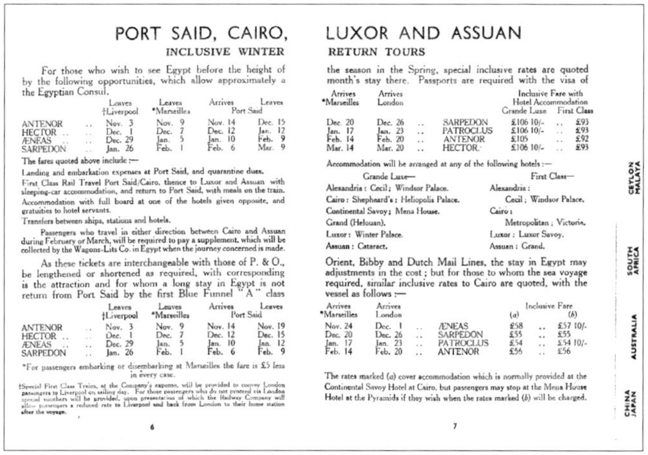

PORT SAID, CAIRO, LUXOR AND ASSUAN

INCLUSIVE WINTER RETURN TOURS

For those who wish to see Egypt before the height of the season in the Spring, special inclusive rates are quoted by the following opportunities, which allow approximately a month's stay there. Passports are required with the visa of the Egyptian Consul.

	Leaves †Liverpool	Leaves *Marseilles	Arrives Port Said	Leaves Port Said	Arrives *Marseilles	Arrives London		Inclusive Fare with Hotel Accommodation: Grande Luxe	First Class
ANTENOR	Nov. 3	Nov. 9	Nov. 14	Dec. 15	Dec. 20	Dec. 26	SARPEDON	£106 10/-	£93
HECTOR	Dec. 1	Dec. 7	Dec. 12	Jan. 12	Jan. 17	Jan. 23	PATROCLUS	£106 10/-	£93
ÆNEAS	Dec. 29	Jan. 5	Jan. 10	Feb. 9	Feb. 14	Feb. 20	ANTENOR	£105	£92
SARPEDON	Jan. 26	Feb. 1	Feb. 6	Mar. 9	Mar. 14	Mar. 20	HECTOR	£106 10/-	£93

The fares quoted above include :—

Landing and embarkation expenses at Port Said, and quarantine dues.

First Class Rail Travel Port Said/Cairo, thence to Luxor and Assuan with sleeping-car accommodation, and return to Port Said, with meals on the train.

Accommodation with full board at one of the hotels given opposite, and gratuities to hotel servants.

Transfers between ships, stations and hotels.

Passengers who travel in either direction between Cairo and Assuan during February or March, will be required to pay a supplement, which will be collected by the Wagons-Lits Co. in Egypt when the journey concerned is made.

Accommodation will be arranged at any of the following hotels :—

Grande Luxe—	First Class—
Alexandria : Cecil ; Windsor Palace.	Alexandria : Cecil ; Windsor Palace.
Cairo : Shepheard's ; Heliopolis Palace. Continental Savoy ; Mena House. Grand (Helouan).	Cairo : Metropolitan ; Victoria.
Luxor : Winter Palace.	Luxor : Luxor Savoy.
Assuan : Cataract.	Assuan : Grand.

As these tickets are interchangeable with those of P. & O., Orient, Bibby and Dutch Mail Lines, the stay in Egypt may be lengthened or shortened as required, with corresponding adjustments in the cost ; but for those to whom the sea voyage is the attraction and for whom a long stay in Egypt is not required, similar inclusive rates to Cairo are quoted, with the return from Port Said by the first Blue Funnel "A" class vessel as follows :—

	Leaves †Liverpool	Leaves *Marseilles	Arrives Port Said	Leaves Port Said	Arrives *Marseilles	Arrives London		Inclusive Fare (a)	Inclusive Fare (b)
ANTENOR	Nov. 3	Nov. 9	Nov. 14	Nov. 19	Nov. 24	Dec. 1	ÆNEAS	£58	£57 10/-
HECTOR	Dec. 1	Dec. 7	Dec. 12	Dec. 15	Dec. 20	Dec. 26	SARPEDON	£55	£55
ÆNEAS	Dec. 29	Jan. 5	Jan. 10	Jan. 12	Jan. 17	Jan. 23	PATROCLUS	£54	£54 10/-
SARPEDON	Jan. 26	Feb. 1	Feb. 6	Feb. 9	Feb. 14	Feb. 20	ANTENOR	£56	£56

*For passengers embarking or disembarking at Marseilles the fare is £5 less in every case.

†Special First Class Trains, at the Company's expense, will be provided to convey London passengers to Liverpool on sailing day. For those passengers who do not proceed via London special vouchers will be provided, upon presentation of which the Railway Company will allow passengers a reduced rate to Liverpool and back from London to their home station after the voyage.

The rates marked (*a*) cover accommodation which is normally provided at the Continental Savoy Hotel at Cairo, but passengers may stop at the Mena House Hotel at the Pyramids if they wish when the rates marked (*b*) will be charged.

6 7

Right: Anchises (3) looking aft.

Below and opposite: Pages from the 1934-35 brochure.

SOUTH AFRICA

VIA THE CANARY ISLANDS

£75 Winter Return Fare, First Class

The Blue Funnel and White Star Lines offer reduced fares by the undermentioned First Class vessels of their Joint Service to those who wish to spend part of the Winter in the sun of South Africa.

For those travelling outwards and homewards in any of the vessels named, the reduced First Class Return Fare will be from £75, including First Class Railway Fare by the Special Boat Train from London. Passengers disembark at Cape Town, and may return from either Durban or Cape Town without additional charge.

Opportunity is thus given for an ideal holiday of from seven to fourteen weeks' duration, which embodies twenty days at sea each way.

Sailings Outwards	From †Liverpool	Arrives Cape Town
THEMISTOCLES	Nov. 17	Dec. 7
NESTOR	Jan. 5	Jan. 25

†Special First Class Trains, at the Company's expense, will be provided to convey London passengers to Liverpool on sailing day.

10

SOUTH AFRICA

VIA THE CANARY ISLANDS

£75 Winter Return Fare, First Class

Rail Tours, including hotel accommodation, whilst in South Africa can also be arranged, either before departure or upon arrival in South Africa.

These Tours vary from a few hours to several weeks in length, and cover all the renowned places of interest in South Africa and Rhodesia, e.g., Victoria Falls, Zimbabwe Ruins, Diamond Mines, Cango Caves, &c. The itineraries include all train and motor arrangements, and hotel reservations.

Passports are required valid for the British Empire.

From Durban	From Cape Town	Arrives London	Sailings Homewards
Dec. 14	Dec. 19	Jan. 8	ANCHISES
Dec. 28	Jan. 3	Jan. 23	ULYSSES
Jan. 25	Jan. 30	Feb. 19	ASCANIUS

11

SOUTH AFRICA

AUSTRALIA

CHINA JAPAN

ROUND VOYAGES TO AUSTRALIA

VIA THE CANARY ISLANDS AND SOUTH AFRICA

£120 Return, First Class

The Blue Funnel and White Star Lines offer passengers making the Round Voyage to Australia in any of their First Class vessels the above reduced fare, which amounts to less than £30 a month.

The sailing of the NESTOR, whose schedule is detailed below, is an exceptional opportunity, as she sails on January 5th, immediately after the Christmas and New Year festivities, avoids those bleak British months of January, February and March, and brings her passengers back to England at the beginning of May. Schedules of other vessels of the Joint Service will be found on the following page.

NESTOR, 14,628 Tons Gross

Port	Arrives 1935	Leaves 1935	Approximate Time in Port
† Liverpool	—	Sat., Jan. 5	—
Las Palmas	Fri., Jan. 11	Fri., Jan. 11	6 hours
Cape Town	Fri., Jan. 25	Fri., Jan. 25	12 hours
Fremantle	Sat., Feb. 9	Sat., Feb. 9	12 hours
Adelaide	Thurs., Feb. 14	Thurs., Feb. 14	12 hours
Melbourne	Sat., Feb. 16	Tues., Feb. 19	4 days
Sydney	Thurs., Feb. 21	Mon., Feb. 25	5 days
Newcastle	Mon., Feb. 25	Tues., Feb. 26	2 days
Brisbane	Thurs., Feb. 28	Tues., Mar. 5	5 days
Sydney	Thurs., Mar. 7	Sat., Mar. 9	3 days
Hobart	Mon., Mar. 11	Tues., Mar. 12	36 hours
Melbourne	Thurs., Mar. 14	Sat., Mar. 16	2 days
Adelaide	Mon., Mar. 18	Wed., Mar. 20	2½ days
Fremantle	Mon., Mar. 25	Tues., Mar. 26	2 days
Durban	Tues., April 9	Thurs., April 11	2½ days
Cape Town	Sun., April 14	Sun., April 14	12 hours
Las Palmas	Sun., April 28	Sun., April 28	6 hours
United Kingdom	Sat., May 4	—	—

†Special First Class Trains, at the Company's expense, will be provided to convey London passengers to Liverpool on sailing day.

12

VIA THE CANARY ISLANDS AND SOUTH AFRICA

£120 Return, First Class

Passports are required valid for the British Empire.

Passengers making the Round Voyage are allowed a special rate of two-thirds the ordinary fare for any journeys they may make by the Australian Railways.

The Round Voyage rate is available by any of the following vessels on similar itineraries :—

	Gross Tonnage	Leaves †Liverpool 1934	Arrives London 1935
*ASCANIUS	10,048	Oct. 20	Feb. 19
*THEMISTOCLES	11,250	Nov. 17	Mar. 20
NESTOR	14,628	Jan. 5	May 4
ANCHISES	10,000	Feb. 2	June 1
ULYSSES	14,646	Mar. 2	June 29
*ASCANIUS	10,048	Mar. 30	July 27
*THEMISTOCLES	11,250	May 11	Sept. 10
*NESTOR	14,628	June 22	Oct. 19
*ANCHISES	10,000	July 27	Nov. 12
*ULYSSES	14,646	Aug. 10	Dec. 10

* Do not call at Hobart

† Special First Class Trains, at the Company's expense, will be provided to convey London passengers to Liverpool on sailing day.

13

AUSTRALIA

CHINA JAPAN

Left: Stewards playing cricket on *Anchises* (3) well deck.

Above: Passengers relax on *Anchises* (3) boat deck.

Right: In the tropics on *Anchises* (3) boat deck.

Below: Games on the boat deck.

Captain and officers on *Anchises* (3) bridge.

Second and Third Officers.

The Chief Officer and Doctor of *Anchises* (3).

At the outbreak of the Second World War, the company operated seventy-six Blue Funnel and eleven Glen Line vessels with an average age of twenty years and an aggregate gross tonnage of 619,288 tons. Lawrence Holt was appointed senior partner in 1941 on the death of Richard Holt. The company's headquarters at India Buildings in Liverpool was severely damaged following a German air raid on 3 May 1941.

In the Second World War, the Blue Funnel Line lost forty-one ships with a gross tonnage of 321,673 – more than half of their fleet, which was reduced to thirty-six vessels, totalling 292,097 gross tons.

Protesilaus	21.01.40	Mined in the Bristol Channel
Pyrrhus (2)	17.02.40	Torpedoed by U-37 off Cape Finisterre
Teiresias	17.06.40	Bombed off St.Nazaire
Aeneas	2.07.40	Bombed off Plymouth
Titan (2)	4.09.40	Torpedoed by U-47 in Atlantic
Eurymedon (2)	25.09.40	Torpedoed by U-29 in Atlantic
Automedon	11.11.40	Sank by surface raider in Indian Ocean
Patroclus (3)	4.11.40	Torpedoed by U-99 off Northern Ireland
Clytoneus	8.01.41	Bombed and sank south of Rockall
Eumaeus (2)	14.01.41	Torpedoed by Italian submarine off Freetown
Meriones	24.01.41	Bombed off Norfolk coast
Eurylochus	29.01.41	Attacked and sunk off West Africa
Anchises (3)	28.02.41	Sank by aerial bombing in the Irish Sea
Memnon (4)	11.03.41	Torpedoed by U-106 off West Africa
Calchas (2)	21.04.41	Torpedoed by U-107 off West Africa
Ixion (2)	7.05.41	Torpedoed by U-94 in Atlantic
Tantalus (2)	26.12.41	Bombed off Manila
Cyclops (2)	11.01.42	Sunk by U-123 off the East Coast of the United States
Talthybius (2)	6.02.42	Scuttled at Singapore
Helenus	3.03.42	Torpedoed and sunk by U-68 off West Africa
Hector (4)	5.04.42	Bombed and sunk in Colombo Harbour
Dardanus (3)	6.04.42	Shelled and torpedoed by Japanese warship in the Bay of Bengal
Autolycus (2)	6.04.42	Sank by Japanese warship in the Bay of Bengal
Ulysses (4)	11.04.42	Torpedoed by U-160 off Palm Beach
Laertes (3)	3.05.42	Torpedoed by U-564 in Atlantic
Peisander	17.05.42	Torpedoed by U-653 off Nantucket
Polyphemus (3)	26.05.42	Torpedoed U-135 in the Atlantic
Mentor	28.05.42	Torpedoed by U-106 off Key West
Medon	10.08.42	Torpedoed by Italian submarine in the Atlantic
Deucalion (3)	12.08.42	Bombed and torpedoed off Tunisia
Myrmidon (3)	5.09.42	Torpedoed by U-506 off Liberia
Agapenor	11.10.42	Torpedoed by U-87 off West Africa
Stentor (3)	27.10.42	Torpedoed by U-509 off North Africa
Maron	13.11.42	Torpedoed by U-81 between Algiers and Gibraltar
Polydorus	27.11.42	Torpedoed by U-176, 760 miles off Freetown
Rhexenor	3.02.43	Torpedoed by U-217 in the Atlantic
Dolius	5.08.43	Torpedoed by U-638 in the Atlantic
Centaur (2)	14.05.43	Torpedoed by Japanese off the East Coast of Australia
Phemius (2)	19.12.43	Sunk by U-515 off West Africa
Perseus (2)	16.01.44	Torpedoed off Madras by Japanese submarine
Troilus	31.08.44	Torpedoed by U-859 in Indian Ocean

The company took delivery of a number of vessels during the Second World War. *Priam* and *Telemachus* were built in 1942 and 1943 respectively by the Caledon Shipbuilding & Engineering Company at Dundee. The completion of the war saw the purchase of six 'Victory' ships to enable services to be provided and they were renamed *Polyphemus*, *Polydorus*, *Maron*, *Mentor*, *Myrmidon* and *Memnon*. Eight 'Liberty' ships were also purchased, which became *Eurymedon*, *Eumaeus*, *Eurypylus*, *Titan*, *Troilus*, *Talthybius*, *Tydeus* and *Tantalus* and two Empire Rawlinson class were purchased and renamed *Rhexenor* and *Stentor* and *Empire Splendour* was renamed *Medon*.

New ships were being built in various British shipyards. Initially, three classes of vessels were introduced, which were the *Anchises*, *Peleus* and *Helenus* types. The first A-class vessel was *Calchas*, which was built by Harland & Wolff and launched by Mrs Lawrence Holt on 27 August 1946. All of the A class were equipped with eight-cylinder, two-stroke double-acting engines of the Burmeister & Wain coverless design, developing 6,800 bhp, giving a speed of 15 ½ knots. They were designed as two-deck type, with poop, long bridge and forecastle.

Accommodation for twelve passengers was arranged in a deckhouse on the promenade deck and dining room and lounge was provided. They had six cargo holds and 'tween decks, with an additional lower 'tween deck forward, where there was also a strong room for special cargo. Holds number 3 and 4 were constructed for the carriage of 2,250 tons of vegetable oils in five separate tanks. The large hatchways were up to 36 feet in length by 22 feet wide and were served by twenty-four derricks, eight of these lifting 10 tons each, and the remainder suitable for 5-ton lifts; in addition, a 50-ton derrick was fitted at the foremast and a 25-ton derrick at the mainmast, while a 5-ton derrick was provided for engine-room use. The class was also built with twenty-four electric winches and an electric windlass.

A complete system of pre-detecting and fire-extinguishing gear on the CO_2 system was installed. Storerooms for both dry and refrigerated stores were provided while there were also insulated chambers for the carriage of some refrigerated cargo. Navigation equipment included gyrocompass, direction finder, echo sounder, radar and a clear view screen. Each officer had a single-berth cabin and the crew were in two-berth cabins at the after end of the boat deck, and the Asian crew in the poop. Each crew cabin contained two bunks, one of which was arranged fore and aft and the other athwartships, both had draw curtains and an electric reading light. There was a double wardrobe, a chest of drawers, a folding table and a wooden seat. There was a single cabin for the leading seaman and a three-berth cabin for deck boys. There was a smoke-room adjacent to the cabins and a mess-room next to the galley. The Asian seamen in the poop had their own galley and mess-room, and showers,

Gladstone Dock, Liverpool.

Talthybius (3).

Above left: *Asphalion* (2) at Penang.

Above right: *Elpenor* (2) in the East Float at Birkenhead.

Right: *Pyrrhus* (3) in Gladstone Dock, Liverpool.

baths and clothes washing and drying facilities were provided for use by all the crew.

Peleus was a single-screw passenger and cargo vessel propelled by a set of Parsons-type turbines with double-reduction gearing, and steam was provided at 525 lb, and pressure and 850-degree superheat were provided by two Foster Wheeler water-tube boilers. Her normal shaft horsepower was 14,000, which could be increased to 15,000 shp, which was claimed to be the greatest power ever developed on a single screw. Accommodation was provided for twenty-nine first class passengers. *Peleus* carried general cargo, except in number 4 hold and 'tween decks, which were arranged for the carriage of refrigerated cargo. The vessels were subdivided by nine watertight transverse bulkheads to the upper decks. The vessels of the class had six cargo holds, lower and upper 'tween deck, including the refrigerated hold. Deep tanks for cargo oil were built in number 3 hold and lower 'tween decks. Large refrigerated chambers were fitted in the centrecastle, together with general storerooms.

Passenger accommodation consisted of first class staterooms situated on the promenade deck, seven single-berth rooms, each with extra Pullman berth. Three two-berth cabins, two two-berth rooms with extra Pullman

Above left: Coaling at Moji.

Above right: Anchored at Moji.

Helenus was loading at the south side of No. 2 branch Gladstone Dock for her maiden voyage when a fire broke out. *Nestor* was discharging at the north side of the dock and *Helenus* and *Dardanus* were loading at the south side when the fire began. *Pyrrhus* and *Calchas* were also discharging, and *Laomedon* was expected to follow. It was arranged to take an aerial photograph of the group of vessels for the company's house magazine, but the photographer was able to capture the disastrous fire. *Helenus* and *Dardanus* were moved to safer berths, and it was decided to sail *Helenus* on schedule. However, she was unable to sail for two days because of a severe gale.

Helenus-class vessels were designed with well-raked, rounded-stem hulls, cruiser-type sterns, two masts and a single elliptical funnel. There was one complete steel deck, a main deck forward and aft of the machinery space, a lower deck forward of the machinery space and poop, centrecastle, forecastle, promenade and boat decks. There were seven main cargo holds, four forward and three aft of the machinery space, two of the forward holds were used for insulated cargo, and number 5 hold was arranged as a deep tank. Cargo-handling equipment included a 50-ton derrick, four 10-ton derricks, four 7-ton derricks and sixteen 5-ton derricks. The vessels were designed with single-shaft, triple-expansion, double-reduction-geared turbines capable of developing 14,000 shaft horsepower ahead of a propeller speed of 106 rpm, giving a service speed

berth, and one special two-berth room with private bathroom. There was a dining room, lounge, bar and entrance hall lounge. The dining room seated fifty-two people and the entrance hall was an extension to the lounge. Officers were accommodated in a large deckhouse on the boat deck in single rooms with the captain and chief engineer each having a suite with private bathrooms. Seamen and stewards were accommodated in two-berth cabins, situated on the centrecastle deck and after end of the upper deck. There were separate mess-rooms for the various departments, together with a library and recreational room.

The cargo-handling arrangements comprised one 50-ton derrick, one 20-ton derrick, eight 10-ton derricks and sixteen 5-ton derricks served by electric winches. An electric windlass was fitted with other modern items such as electro-hydraulic steering gear, gyroscopic compass, wireless installation, echo-sounding apparatus and radar. A complete smoke-detecting and fire-extinguishing system and ventilation to all accommodation was fitted.

The *Helenus*-class vessels were similar to the *Peleus* class but were built with a higher cargo capacity to allow for 3,500 tons of refrigerated space, as they were intended for the Australian trade. On 9 November 1949,

Discharging a heavy lift at Pukow on the Yangtze.

Course 158 at the Outward Bound Sea School, Aberdovey. April, 1956.

of 18 ½ knots. Two oil-fired Foster Wheeler controlled superheat boilers were also fitted.

There was accommodation for twenty-nine passengers in single- and two-berth cabins, all fitted with cot beds and a Pullman bed in four of the single rooms and two of the two-berth rooms. Ten private bathrooms were provided for the eighteen passenger cabins. Passenger facilities also included an entrance lounge with bar, and a main lounge at the fore end of the promenade deck, whilst a spacious dining room was arranged on the centrecastle deck. Crew accommodation was arranged amidships, and at the after end of the vessels for the Chinese engine-room ratings.

The company instituted their own training scheme for midshipmen, engineers and stewards, and the *Calchas* was used as their training ship until 1956, when the role was transferred to the new *Diomed*.

Malayan Airways Limited was a joint initiative between the Ocean Steamship Company, the Straits Steamship Company and Imperial Airways. It was formed to run an air service between Penang and Singapore, and the

THE BLUE FUNNEL LINE

Alfred Holt & Co., India Buildings, Liverpool 2

AUSTRALIAN SERVICE HOMEWARD

SAIL ARRIVE JANUARY, 1961

VESSEL	FINAL PORT		Genoa	Dunkirk	Antwerp	Liverpool	Glasgow	Other Discharge Ports
IXION	Sydney	Dec. 6	—	Jan. 3	Jan. 5	Jan. 8	Jan. 14	
JASON	Brisbane	Jan. 3	—	Feb. 2	Feb. 4	Feb. 8	Feb. 15	
NESTOR	Melbourne	Jan. 11	—	Feb. 9	Feb. 11	Feb. 15	Feb. 22	
HELENUS	Fremantle	Feb. 4	—	Feb. 28	Mar. 2	Mar. 5	Mar. 11	
NELEUS	Sydney	Feb. 11	—	Mar. 15	Mar. 17	Mar. 19	Mar. 25	
HECTOR	Adelaide	Mar. 11	—	Apr. 7	Apr. 9	Apr. 12	Apr. 19	
RHEXENOR	Sydney	Mar. 24	(Apr. 22)	(Apr. 27)	(Apr. 28)	Apr. 30	May 6	

Above: The crew of *Diomed* at Otaru, Japan on 10 May 1958.

Right: Australian service sailing schedule, 1961.

first commercial flight took place from Singapore to Kuala Lumpur on 2 April 1947. This was followed by regular weekly flights from Singapore to Ipoh, Penang, Kuala Lumpur, Jakarta, Medan, Palembang and Saigon.

Douglas DC-3 aircraft were introduced into the fleet in the 1950s, and the name was changed to Malaysian Airlines in 1963 when Malaya, Singapore, Sabah and Sarawak formed the Federation of Malaysia. It became Malaysia-Singapore Airlines in 1966 and was separated into Malaysian Airlines System and Singapore Airlines in 1972. Both airlines expanded and operated both domestic and international services from their bases at Kuala Lumpur and Singapore.

Tyndareus was converted to a pilgrim ship in 1949 to carry up to 2,200 people between South-East Asia and Jeddah two or three times a year and the Australian passenger service was terminated in 1950. *Pyrrhus* was nearly lost by fire at Liverpool in 1964. It took a full day to control the blaze and she was later repaired and continued in service.

In 1951, Elder Dempster purchased the fleet of ten ships owned by Henderson's British & Burmese Steam Navigation Company, and in 1953, the name of Elder Dempster Lines Holdings was changed to Liner Holdings. The Ocean Steamship Company would go on to acquire all the ordinary shares in Liner Holdings in 1965.

Lawrence Holt retired in 1953, after a career lasting forty-five years with the company. He had also been a director of the Caledon Shipbuilding & Engineering Company, Glen Line, Elder Dempster and Scott's Shipbuilding & Engineering Company. He was the son of Robert Durning Holt and was educated at the Drapers Preparatory School, Lockers, Hemel Hempstead, and at Winchester. On 24 September 1900, he started work as an office boy at the offices of Alfred Booth & Company in Liverpool. Four years later, he joined the Ocean Steamship Company, and in 1907, at the age of twenty-five, he was made a partner of the company.

Lawrence Holt travelled the world in the ships of the Blue Funnel Line and took an interest in the welfare of the seafarers employed by the company.

Above left: Blue Funnel postcard.

Above right: *Gunung Djati.*

Left: Centaur (3).

When war was declared in 1939, he was responsible for ensuring that every officer and seaman should be proficient in lifeboat drill and procedure. A full-sized model of a lifeboat was set up in a dock shed and was used to train the staff in its use in an emergency. His extensive knowledge of different trades and commodities carried by the line helped in its success over the years he was a partner. A dinner was held in his honour by retired masters and engineers at the Adelphi Hotel in Liverpool in 1951, when they presented him with an illuminated address signed by the seafarers. It said:

> To Lawrence Durning Holt Esq.
>
> We retired masters and chief engineers, freely give our duty, our loyalty and our affection. Whether, when we sailed in ships of the Blue Funnel Line or now that we have come to our moorings ashore, he has given us always understanding, friendship and his trust. In the example of his word and deed, his leadership has inspired us to keep faith with him and our motto *Certum pete finem.*

He was chairman of the management of the school-ship *Conway* from 1934 and also took an interest in the Outward Bound Sea School at Aberdovey. He was leader of the Liberal Party in Liverpool and was elected Lord Mayor of the City in 1929. He was a Justice of the Peace, chairman of the Local Employment Committee in 1918, Dock Labour Joint Committee up to 1929, member of the Coal Mines Reorganisation Commission, Imperial Communications Inquiry Committee, and of Lord Fleming's Tribunal,

THE BLUE FUNNEL, GLEN AND SHIRE LINES

OCEAN STEAM SHIP CO. LTD. THE CHINA MUTUAL STEAM NAVIGATION CO. LTD. GLEN LINE LTD.

APPROXIMATE SCHEDULE OF EASTERN PASSENGER SERVICE SAILINGS

1961

Subject to alteration without notice

SHIP	Leaves U.K. or Continent	Due Port Said	Due Penang	Due Singapore	Due Manila	Due Hong Kong	Due Japan
§ GLENEARN ...	Jan. 4	Jan. 12	Jan. 26	Feb. 1	—	Feb. 7	Feb. 18
† PELEUS* ...	Jan. 7	Jan. 21	—	Feb. 3	Feb. 9	Feb. 14	Feb. 20
† AUTOMEDON	Jan. 10	Jan. 19	Feb. 2	Feb. 4	B —	Feb. 21	—
§ GLENSHIEL ...	Jan. 11	Jan. 20	—	Feb. 4	B Feb. 21	Feb. 19	—
† ADRASTUS ...	Jan. 18	Jan. 27	Feb. 10	Feb. 15	—	Feb. 21	Feb. 27
† ACHILLES* ...	Jan. 20	Feb. 2	—	Feb. 16	B —	—	—
§ CARDIGAN-SHIRE ...	Jan. 20	Jan. 28	Feb. 11	Feb. 17	—	Feb. 23	Mar. 6
† POLYDORUS ...	Jan. 24	Feb. 2	Feb. 16	Feb. 21	—	Feb. 27	Mar. 5
† AUTOLYCUS ..	Feb. 1	Feb. 10	Feb. 24	Mar. 1	—	Mar. 7	—
§ GLENROY ..	Feb. 4	Feb. 12	Feb. 26	Mar. 4	—	Mar. 10	Mar. 21
‡ CYCLOPS ..	Feb. 4	Feb. 15	Mar. 1	Mar. 8	I —	—	—
† PATROCLUS* ...	Feb. 7	Feb. 21	—	Mar. 6	Mar. 12	Mar. 17	Mar. 23
† ANTILOCHUS	Feb. 8	Feb. 17	Mar. 5	Mar. 12	I —	—	—
† MENESTHEUS	Feb. 11	Feb. 20	—	Mar. 6	B —	Mar. 20	—
† MENELAUS ...	Feb. 18	Feb. 27	Mar. 12	Mar. 17	—	Mar. 23	Mar. 29
† DEMODOCUS*	Feb. 20	Mar. 5	—	Mar. 19	B —	—	—
§ GLENGYLE ...	Feb. 20	Feb. 28	Mar. 14	Mar. 20	—	Mar. 26	Apr. 6
† ATREUS ...	Feb. 24	Mar. 5	Mar. 19	Mar. 24	—	Mar. 30	Apr. 5
† DOLIUS ...	Mar. 1	Mar. 10	Mar. 23	Mar. 28	—	Apr. 3	—
§ DENBIGHSHIRE	Mar. 4	Mar. 12	Mar. 26	Apr. 1	—	Apr. 7	Apr. 18
† PERSEUS* ...	Mar. 7	Mar. 21	—	Apr. 3	Apr. 9	Apr. 14	Apr. 20
† LAOMEDON ...	Mar. 8	Mar. 17	Apr. 2	Apr. 9	I —	—	—
† MACHAON ...	Mar. 11	Mar. 20	—	Apr. 3	B —	Apr. 17	—
§ GLENFRUIN ...	Mar. 11	Mar. 20	—	Apr. 4	B Apr. 21	Apr. 19	—
† DIOMED ...	Mar. 18	Mar. 27	Apr. 9	Apr. 14	—	Apr. 20	Apr. 26
‡ CLYTONEUS ...	Mar. 18	Mar. 27	Apr. 10	Apr. 17	I —	—	—
† ANTENOR* ...	Mar. 20	Apr. 2	—	Apr. 16	B —	—	—
§ GLENARTNEY	Mar. 20	Mar. 28	Apr. 11	Apr. 17	—	Apr. 23	May 4
† AGAPENOR ...	Mar. 24	Apr. 2	Apr. 16	Apr. 21	—	Apr. 27	May 3
† LYCAON ...	Apr. 1	Apr. 10	Apr. 24	Apr. 29	—	May 5	—
§ GLENORCHY ...	Apr. 4	Apr. 12	Apr. 26	May 2	—	May 6	May 17
† PYRRHUS* ...	Apr. 7	Apr. 21	—	May 4	May 10	May 15	May 21
† MEMNON ...	Apr. 11	Apr. 20	—	May 4	B —	May 18	—
§ GLENFINLAS ...	Apr. 11	Apr. 20	—	May 5	B May 22	May 20	—
† LAERTES ...	Apr. 18	Apr. 27	May 11	May 16	—	May 22	May 28
† MELAMPUS* ...	Apr. 20	May 3	—	May 17	B —	—	—
§ BRECONSHIRE	Apr. 20	Apr. 28	May 12	May 18	—	May 24	June 4
† ANCHISES ...	Apr. 24	May 3	May 17	May 22	—	May 28	June 3
† AJAX ...	May 1	May 10	May 23	May 28	—	June 3	—

SHIP	Leaves U.K. or Continent	Due Port Said	Due Penang	Due Singapore	Due Manila	Due Hong Kong	Due Japan
§ GLENGARRY ...	May 4	May 12	May 26	June 1	—	June 7	June 18
† PELEUS* ...	May 6	May 21	—	June 3	June 9	June 14	June 20
† ELPENOR ...	May 8	May 17	May 31	June 7	I —	—	—
† MARON ...	May 11	May 20	—	June 3	B —	June 17	—
§ RADNORSHIRE	May 11	May 20	—	June 4	B June 21	June 19	—
† EUMAEUS ...	May 18	May 27	June 10	June 15	—	June 21	June 27
† AUTOMEDON*	May 20	June 2	—	June 17	B —	—	—
§ GLENEARN ...	May 20	May 28	June 11	June 17	—	June 23	July 4
‡ AENEAS ...	May 20	May 29	June 12	June 19	I —	—	—
† POLYDORUS ...	May 24	June 2	June 16	June 21	—	June 27	July 3
† ADRASTUS ...	June 1	June 10	June 24	June 29	—	July 5	—
§ CARDIGAN-SHIRE ...	June 4	June 12	June 26	July 2	—	July 8	July 19
† PATROCLUS*	June 7	June 21	—	July 4	July 10	July 15	July 21
† ASCANIUS ...	June 8	June 17	July 1	July 8	I —	—	—
† ACHILLES ...	June 10	June 19	—	July 3	B —	July 17	—
§ GLENSHIEL ...	June 11	June 20	—	July 5	B July 22	July 20	—
† AUTOLYCUS ...	June 17	June 26	July 10	July 15	—	July 21	July 27
† MENESTHEUS*	June 20	July 3	—	July 17	B —	—	—
§ GLENROY ...	June 20	June 28	July 12	July 18	—	July 24	Aug. 4
† ATREUS ...	June 24	July 3	July 17	July 22	—	July 28	Aug. 3
† MENELAUS ...	July 1	July 10	July 23	July 28	—	Aug. 3	—
‡ ANTILOCHUS	July 3	July 12	July 26	Aug. 2	I —	—	—
§ GLENGYLE ...	July 4	July 12	July 26	Aug. 1	—	Aug. 7	Aug. 18
† PERSEUS* ...	July 7	July 21	—	Aug. 3	Aug. 9	Aug. 14	Aug. 20
† CYCLOPS ...	July 8	July 17	July 31	Aug. 7	I —	—	—
† DEMODOCUS	July 11	July 20	—	Aug. 3	B —	Aug. 17	—
† DOLIUS ...	July 18	July 27	Aug. 9	Aug. 14	—	Aug. 20	Aug. 26
§ DENBIGHSHIRE	July 20	July 28	Aug. 11	Aug. 17	—	Aug. 23	Sept. 3
† MACHAON*	July 20	Aug. 2	—	Aug. 16	B —	—	—
† AGAPENOR ...	July 24	Aug. 2	Aug. 16	Aug. 21	—	Aug. 27	Sept. 2
† DIOMED ...	Aug. 1	Aug. 10	Aug. 23	Aug. 28	—	Sept. 3	—
§ GLENARTNEY	Aug. 4	Aug. 12	Aug. 26	Sept. 1	—	Sept. 7	Sept. 18
† PYRRHUS* ...	Aug. 5	Aug. 21	—	Sept. 3	Sept. 9	Sept. 14	Sept. 20
† ANTENOR ...	Aug. 11	Aug. 20	—	Sept. 3	B —	—	—
§ GLENFRUIN ...	Aug. 11	Aug. 20	—	Sept. 4	B Sept. 21	Sept. 19	—
† LYCAON ...	Aug. 18	Aug. 27	Sept. 10	Sept. 15	—	Sept. 21	Sept. 27
§ GLENORCHY ...	Aug. 20	Aug. 28	Sept. 11	Sept. 17	—	Sept. 23	Oct. 4
† MEMNON* ...	Aug. 19	Sept. 1	—	Sept. 15	B —	—	—
† ANCHISES ...	Aug. 24	Sept. 2	Sept. 16	Sept. 21	—	Sept. 27	Oct. 3

† *Blue Funnel ships sailing from Birkenhead.*

‡ *Blue Funnel ships sailing from Amsterdam.*

* *Via Rotterdam.*

§ *Glen Line ships sailing from London.*

I *Takes passengers to Indonesia.*

B *Via Bangkok.*

No. 117 JANUARY, 1961

PRINTED IN ENGLAND 1 85M

Blue Funnel, Glen and Shire Lines sailing list, 1961.

The following is quoted from *Halfdeck Magazine*, Vol. 7, January 1958:

Now that the sons of former Midshipmen are joining us in increasing numbers it is no exaggeration to say that generations of Blue Funnel Midshipmen have walked down Riversdale Road to make a temporary home in the Hostel. One wonders what their fathers would say if they could see 'Holm Lea' as it now stands. They will recall a semi-detached house, set among trees at the end of a quiet road, almost a country lane leading down to the river. Two bedrooms, a sitting room and a dining room housed those midshipmen who, for over thirty years, comprised the ever-changing population of 'Holm Lea' and it is a fitting comment on the success of the old hostel that visitors are still to be seen en route for the house and anxious to revisit the scene of earlier experiences. Today the setting is still attractive but the rural peace has gone. A new Technical College across the road provides us with the roar of motorcycles and a litter problem; crowds now use the road as their shortest route to the promenade, and although still twenty minutes by bus to India Buildings, we know the city is moving in around us. The house itself has more than doubled in size and can accommodate over twenty midshipmen. There is room for recreation and study in addition to the essential space required for sleeping, eating and washing.

The first plans for this extensive re-building programme were made when it became apparent that the number of Midshipmen was likely to increase considerably. The opportunity was not found however until the house next door to 'Holm Lea' became vacant, when we were allowed to go ahead with actual construction.

This consisted briefly of building a two-storey link to join the two houses, modifying the size and shape of several existing rooms and providing central heating and new plumbing arrangements. The job was completed within eight months and we can fairly claim to be in business again in a larger, but let us hope, not a more impersonal way. 'Holm Lea' no matter what size, or shape, exists to provide a home for Midshipmen whose duties keep them in Liverpool. It is the foundation of the training scheme for without a base to work from it would not be possible to use to such great advantage the training facilities of Merseyside. The lifeboat School and E.D.H. School, the Radar and Fire-fighting courses, the Rigging Loft and Company's classroom – all these are in daily use and there is a direct relationship between the number of beds at 'Holm Lea' and the efficiency of the training available to our future officers. The new hostel by providing accommodation for increased numbers under training is already making a big contribution to the future efficiency of the fleet.

We were recently visited by Mr Bowes, Director of the Pacific Steam Navigation Co. and Mr Gawne, the Company's Secretary. As the guests of Mr George Holt they dined at 'Holm Lea' and discussed various aspects of training for the sea. After dinner they, and the Midshipmen present, were entertained by Dr Lamb of *Diomed* who projected his film of *Calchas* and *Diomed* activities.

Other visitors included Mrs Spikins and Mrs Asman whom many older Midshipmen will remember from the days when they were our Housekeepers. Mr Jackson, Mr Lumbard, Mr Bowden and Mr Dick, Chief Officers, visited 'Holm Lea' during the day spent in the Midshipmen's Department and we were glad to welcome Mrs Lumbard also. Mr Lumbard was a Midshipman in 1946 and Bosun's Mate of *Calchas*.

Aulis was opened on 18 September 1963 by Mrs Lawrence Holt. The three-storey building stood on the site of the Midshipmen's Hostel and was designed to accommodate 110 midshipmen and engineer cadets. The length of the courses varied from six months for midshipmen, to two years for engineer cadets. The students were accommodated in dormitories and various dayrooms including a large assembly room which was used for recreation, cinema, dancing, and as a lecture hall. There was a library, workshops, and a photographic darkroom. It stood next to the company's playing fields across the road from the Riversdale Technical College.

These pages and overleaf: Alfred Holt postcards.

Tantalus (4) and *Priam* (5) in Gladstone Dock, Liverpool.

Oxford University and the Ministry of Agriculture, chairman of the Liverpool Steamship Owners' Association in 1935-36, trustee of the National Maritime Museum until 1944, and life governor of the Marine Society from 1945.

He was succeeded by Sir John Richard Hobhouse, who was the third son of the Rt Hon. Henry Hobhouse of Hadspen, Somerset. He was educated at Eton and Oxford, and during the First World War, he served with the RGA in the rank of captain and was awarded the Military Cross at Ypres in 1917. He had been a partner since 1920 and had been a member of the National Maritime Board, chairman of the Employers Association of the Port of Liverpool and a vice-chairman of the National Association of Port Employees.

He was treasurer of the University of Liverpool between 1942 and 1948 and was then elected president of the council and Pro-Chancellor. He became chairman of the Liverpool Steamship Owners' Association between 1941 and 1943 and chairman of the General Council of British Shipping between 1942 to 1943. At the outset of war, John Hobhouse became Deputy Commissioner for the North Western Region under the Civil Defence scheme and resigned this position in 1940. Appointed regional representative of the Ministry of War Transport in 1941, he succeeded the late Lord Essendon as chairman of the British Liner Committee in 1944. He was appointed a Justice of the Peace for Liverpool in 1929 and was knighted in 1946.

Helenus was followed by *Jason* and *Hector* in 1950 and *Ixion* in 1951. *Nestor*, *Theseus* and *Neleus* were followed by the first of the M-class vessels, *Menelaus*, in 1957. The company's postwar rebuilding programme was completed in 1960 with the delivery of the last of forty-four ships and *Gunung Djati* replaced *Tyndareus* as the line's pilgrim ship. The Malaya-Indonesia Line

Ocean Steam Ship Group advert.

commenced operations in 1960, providing services from the United States Gulf and North Atlantic ports to Malaya, Singapore and Indonesia. A decision was made in 1961 to reverse the policy that the company would be responsible for the financial risk on its vessels and the passenger service to the Far East was withdrawn the following year. *Melampus* was trapped in the Great Bitter Lake in 1967 together with *Agapenor*. They were released from the Suez Canal in 1975 and later sold by the insurer to Greek and Panamanian owners.

The importance the Blue Funnel Line gave to training was reflected in the opening of new training and residential facilities in Liverpool in 1963. When midshipmen were between ships, they attended the company's head office at India Buildings in Liverpool and had to carry out office work. Those not residing in Merseyside were expected to stay in the hostel in Riverside Road in Liverpool. The hostel was run by two widows, Mrs Spikins and Mrs Hotchkiss, for many years. The head of the midshipmen's department lived in the adjoining property and the senior midshipman had to report to him every night at 2200 hours confirming that all the boys were inside. Daily household

FAR EAST — LIVERPOOL SERVICE

Vessel	DEPART Japan	China	Manila	Sarawak	Hong Kong	Malaya Last Port	Trinco-malee	Colombo	ARRIVE Port Said	French Ports	Liverpool	Dublin	Glasgow	Avonmouth	Ha
ACHAON	—	Shanghai Dec 11	—	Dec 24	—	Jan 6	Jan 12	Jan 14	Jan 23	Havre Feb 1	Feb 4	Feb 12	—	—	F
OLIUS	Dec 24	—	—	—	Jan 1	Jan 11	–	—	Jan 24	—	Feb 2	Feb 10	—	—	
ERSEUS	Dec 31	—	—	—	Jan 7	Jan 18		Jan 21	Jan 30	—	Feb 7	—	Feb 16	—	
IOMED	Dec 29	Hsinkang Dec 22	Jan 4	Jan 10	—	Jan 22	—	Jan 27	Feb 6	Marseilles Feb 11	Feb 17	—	—	Feb 24	
NTENOR	—	—	—	—	Jan 17	Feb 1	—	Feb 7	Feb 16	—	Feb 25	—	Mar 5	—	
EMNON	—	Shanghai Jan 4	Masinloc Jan 8	Jan 18	Labuan Jan 13	Feb 6	Feb 11	Feb 13	Feb 23	Havre Mar 19	Mar 4	Mar 12	—	(Newport Mar 15)	M
YCAON	Jan 25	—	—	—	Feb 2	Feb 10	—	—	Feb 23	—	Mar 4	Mar 12	—	—	
PYRRHUS	Feb 2	—	—	—	Feb 6	Feb 17	—	Feb 21	Mar 2	—	Mar 10	—	Mar 19	—	
AERTES	Jan 25	N.Borneo Feb 1	—	Feb 8	—	Feb 22	–	Feb 27	Mar 9	Marseilles Mar 14	Mar 21	—	—	Mar 28	
NCHISES	Feb 6	—	—	—	Feb 14	Mar 1		Mar 6	Mar 17	—	Mar 26	—	Apr 5	—	
MARON	Bangkok Jan 24	Shanghai Feb 10	Feb 15	Feb 21	—	Mar 6	Mar 11	Mar 13	Mar 23	Havre Apr 15	Apr 1	Apr 12	—	—	A
AJAX	Feb 22	—	—	—	Feb 28	Mar 10	–	—	Mar 23	—	Apr 1	Apr 11	—	—	
PELEUS	Mar 2	—	—	—	Mar 6	Mar 18	–	Mar 22	Mar 31	—	Apr 8	—	Apr 16	—	
EUMAEUS	Otaru Feb 25	Hsinkang Feb 20	Mar 4	Mar 10	—	Mar 22	—	Mar 27	Apr 6	Marseilles Apr 11	Apr 18	—	—	Apr 25	
ADRASTUS	Yokohama Mar 9	—	—	—	Mar 17	Apr 1	–	Apr 6	Apr 16	—	Apr 25	—	May 3	—	
ACHILLES	Bangkok Feb 26	Shanghai Mar 15	Mar 20	Mar 25	—	Apr 6	Apr 11	Apr 13	Apr 23	Havre May 13	May 2	May 10	—	—	M
POLYDORUS	Mar 22	—	—	—	Mar 30	Apr 10	—	—	Apr 24	—	May 3	May 11	—	—	
PATROCLUS	Apr 2	—	—	—	Apr 6	Apr 18	—	Apr 22	May 1	—	May 9	—	May 17	—	
AUTOLYCUS	Otaru Mar 27	Hsinkang Mar 21	Apr 3	Apr 9	–	Apr 22	–	Apr 27	May 7	Marseilles May 12	May 19	—	—	May 27	

Sailing list, 1961.

Clytoneus (2) passing through the Four Bridges at Birkenhead.

The *Diomed* Rugby Team beat Singapore Recreational Club 11-6 on 6 January 1958.

A call at Port Said in November 1957.

tasks and gardening duties were completed and uniforms were worn at all times. The new training unit was built next to the original hostel and included a chartroom, lecture theatre, seamanship room, library, classrooms and dormitory accommodation for midshipmen and engineer cadets and it was named *Aulis*. It was situated next to Elder Dempster's training establishment, River House, and following the merger of the lines in 1975, the two units were merged into one establishment with 280 berths. However, when *Aulis* was opened, it was decided that *Diomed* would not continue as the designated training vessel.

The Malaya-Indonesia Line was renamed the Blue Sea Line and a unique vessel was delivered to the Blue Funnel Line in 1964. *Centaur* was built at John Brown's yard on the Clyde for the Singapore to Fremantle service and was able to carry 188 passengers and 4,500 sheep. She had five holds served by ten derricks and three cranes and a refrigerated capacity of 1,330 cubic metres. *Centaur* was powered by Burmeister & Wain engines, giving a service speed of 18 knots.

On 1 January 1965, the Ocean Steamship Company acquired all the ordinary shares in Liner Holdings, and later that year, they also acquired the Guinea Gulf Line. The company became a publicly quoted company in March 1965, and Sir John Nicholson became the first chairman. Sir John had been a manager since 1944 and Senior Partner since 1957. Liner Holdings became a wholly owned subsidiary of the company in 1965.

An indication of how the Blue Funnel Line was regarded by the people of Merseyside was given in January 1966, when over 15,000 people attended an exhibition organised by the line at the Williamson Art Gallery and Museum at Birkenhead. This was over three times the number that had originally been expected. The exhibition included models of Blue Funnel ships, paintings, drawings, and was the most successful ever held at the museum.

At the annual dinner of the Blue Funnel Reunion Association in 1966 Sir Stewart Mactier, a director of the Ocean Steamship Company said the new *Priam*-class ships would show that the company had to design ships which were capable of fast cargo working and which were simple to run and maintain. He said that he believed that in the 'Priams', they had found many answers to these problems, but conditions were changing very quickly, which called for a large degree of gazing in the crystal ball. He said that, as they gaze into this crystal ball, they find that the vision is obscured to a pretty alarming extent by political, commercial and industrial fog.

Priam was built in 1966 and was the first of the final class of conventional cargo vessels to be designed and built for the Blue Funnel Line. They were vastly different in appearance to the older classes with the forecastle, bridge and poop standing out in sharp profile. She was designed with a long forecastle encompassing No. 1 hatch, as well as a deck with four hatches, and a long poop, which carried the accommodation block. The *Priam* class were designed to carry general cargo, refrigerated goods, liquids, and some containerised cargo. The dry cargo spaces were all air-conditioned and dehumidified.

The crew complement consisted of forty-three officers and men,

M.V. "DIOMED" WORKING ROUTINE.

The ship is manned by 22 Midshipmen, eleven "Seniors" and eleven "Juniors", a senior being one who has made a voyage already in the ship, a junior one who is making his first voyage in the ship.

The Bosun's Mate and Lamptrimmer are always two of the senior eleven. The amount of Sea time that each boy has, has nothing to do with his status in this ship. In other words if he has done one voyage in the ship he is a senior, if he has not done a voyage in the ship he is a junior, irrespective of how much sea time he has in.

Of the senior eleven two are the Bosun's Mate and Lamptrimmer. Two are the 5th and 6th Mates, this is to say they work with the 2nd and 3rd Mates at sea and in port doing all the duties that those two officers do and taking their meals in the saloon, with these officers when they do. The 5th and 6th Mates change each week. Of the remaining seniors - three are on watch and four are daymen.

Of the junior eleven - there are two in each watch, three daymen, an Accommodation "peggy" and a Mess "peggy". Of the latter two the Accommodation peggy works in accommodation until 10.00 a.m. each day and then joins the daymnen. The mess peggy does no other job other than the mess.

When entering and leaving port the Bosun's Mate goes forward and the Lamptrimmer aft. The watch on deck supply wheel, gangway and lookout. The last watch on standby the forward springs. The next watch on standby the after springs, and of the daymen - two seniors and two juniors for forward, two seniors and two juniors go aft, leaving the mess peggy who stands by down in the Engine Room.

In port when the ship is working there are at least five men aboard at all times. Either the 5th or 6th mate, the gangwayman and a derrick gang of three. One senior, and two juniors. With the exception of the two leading hands, all the duties are changed once a week – ie :- On Sunday.

In addition to the 5th and 6th Mates who always dine in the Saloon, the two juniors of the 8 - 12 watch always have dinner in the Saloon at sea, thus ensuring that all midshipmen dine with the officers from time to time.

The new Bosun's Mate and Lamptrimmer for the next voyage are selected at Singapore homeward. For two weeks (usually between Port Swettenham and Colombo) these two leading hands assume control for a trial fortnight. This has been found to be a great help when they take up their new duties the next voyage. When the two newly selected leading hands take over, the two old ones become 5th and 6th Mates thus getting in their "Bridge Time". At the end of the trial fortnight, the old leading hands revert but the two newly selected ones, although not in charge, shadow their seniors and remain on day work for the remainder of the voyage.

On arrival at the first U.K. port as a rule all midshipmen proceed on leave. For coasting the old senior and the new junior eleven coast, thus leaving the old junior eleven (*or* as they are now, the new senior eleven) time to get in their leave.

It is clearly understood that if a Bosun's Mate or Lamptrimmer proves unsatisfactory he can be disrated and replaced. This has occurred in the past.

A Landing Book is supplied and should be filled in by all midshipmen going ashore and also when they return to the ship. Similarly there is a Sailing Book to be filled up each time a dinghy is taken away. The standing Orders concerning shore leave and sailing are contained in these hooks.

If a midshipmen wishes to change his watch he must first get permission from the Chief Officer.

A. Holt & Co

Alfred Holt Working Routine.

Deck sports in the tropics.

Above left: R. G. Pritchard in the bosun's chair applying white lead and tallow to the funnel staging.

Above right: Loading logs at Bohihan Island.

Clytoneus (2) on trials in 1948.

Right: The Deck Boys' Training School at the Odyssey Works in Corporation Road, Birkenhead, was established to give the boys some practical training. The young men had been sent to the Outward Bound School at Aberdovey for training in the deck and stewards departments. The six-week course covered knots, splicing of rope and wire, parts of a ship, ship routine and watch-keeping. Practical work was carried out on the ships that were loading in Vittoria Dock and lifeboat procedures were taught in lifeboats in the dock. A large classroom and office was opened in 1958 and a number of large-scale working models were constructed in the joiner's shop. 'British Ropes' presented the best student in each course with a package containing a sheath knife, marlin spike, sewing palm and needles, which was presented by Mr G. P. Holt on several occasions. The Deck Boy students were usually accommodated at the Birkenhead YMCA and were given pocket money. The training course was extended and acquired more classroom space and equipment. Fire-fighting and life-saving training was included and there was an identified need for lessons in English and arithmetic. A mock-up of a wheelhouse was built with a life-size working lifeboat with gravity davits on a deck that could be tilted to simulate a listing vessel. As the size of the fleet declined, the demand for courses was reduced and the school was closed in 1972.

BLUE FUNNEL

When the new quota period for Hong Kong textiles begins on 1st February, 1961, there may be many Importers requiring earliest possible shipment and delivery of their goods. To meet this, and to assist Importers in making early plans with their suppliers, Blue Funnel have arranged to have three vessels on the berth in the first half of February.

	AT HONG KONG	ARRIVES LIVERPOOL
Lycaon	27th January - 2nd February	6th March
Pyrrhus	5th February - 6th February	11th March
Anchises	12th February - 16th February	26th March

ALFRED HOLT & CO., INDIA BUILDINGS, LIVERPOOL 2. PHONE: CENTRAL 5630
BUTTERFIELD & SWIRE (HONG KONG) LTD., UNION HOUSE, 9 CONNAUGHT ROAD, HONG KONG. PHONE 35711

Above: Blue Funnel notice to shippers in 1961.

Left: The 'new' loading sheds at Vittoria Dock, Birkenhead, in 1967.

Top: Tantalus (3) unloading at Liverpool.

Above: Mentor (2) aground at Garvel Point, Greenock, on 31 October 1965 (James Barron).

Right: The loading berths at Gladstone Dock, Liverpool

Construction of the loading berths at Vittoria Dock, Birkenhead.

A busy scene in the River Mersey in 1970.

Lycaon (3).

Above: Centaur (3).

Right: Kowloon Bay in dry dock at Singapore after grounding off Sumatra, Indonesia on 24 November 1989.

which was the result of a task analysis by the line, and the entire engineering installation was designed to be operated by one officer in the control room whilst at sea and could be unattended when in port. Crew accommodation was based on single-berth cabins and was completely air-conditioned. The bridge was fitted with duplicated radar sets, automatic helmsman, long- and medium-range radio-telegraph and radio equipment, complete intercom throughout the accommodation and operating points, answer-back telephones between bridge and all control points. Six of the class were propelled by nine-cylinder 84-VT2BF18Q Burmester & Wain engines and two of the class by nine-cylinder RD90 Mitsubishi-Sulzer engines, designed to develop 18,900 shp at 110 rpm. *Priam*'s B&W engine was built in Copenhagen and installed on the Tyne, where she was constructed.

The class was handed over at the start of the container revolution and had a very short life with the company. *Priam*, *Peisander*, *Prometheus* and *Protesilaus* were sold to the C. Y. Tung Orient Overseas Line in 1978-79. Four other vessels of the *Priam* class were allocated to the Glen Line as *Radnorshire*, *Glenfinlas*, *Pembrokeshire* and *Glenalmond*. The Six-Day War in the Middle East closed the Suez Canal in 1967 and *Melampus* (11) and *Agapenor* (11) were trapped in the Great Bitter Lake.

A major financial commitment to new loading berths and facilities was completed at Vittoria Dock at Birkenhead in 1967. This complex was built in conjunction with the Mersey Docks & Harbour Board and cost £1.5 million. Blue Funnel Line was operating eight sailings a month from Birkenhead to the Far East when these new berths were opened and claimed that this was the most modern dock in Europe.

The name of Alfred Holt & Company was changed to Ocean Fleets Limited in 1967, and in 1972, the ships became the responsibility of various divisions of Ocean Transport & Trading Company. Ships were regularly transferred between lines in this period and traditional 'Blue Funnel' ships were seen in West African ports.

The Australian Government made it clear that they would welcome the introduction of containerisation in services, and the company was involved in the creation of Overseas Containers Limited (OCL) in 1965, owning a 19 per cent share in the organisation. OCL commenced operations in 1969, and by the early 1970s, Ocean's share in it increased to 49 per cent. Following a major restructuring, the line was divided into the Blue Funnel Line, Elder Dempster Lines, Glen Line and the Nederlandsche Stoomvaart Maatschappij 'Oceaan'. In 1969, a joint venture between the Ocean Steamship Company and P&O called Panocean Shipping & Trading was established. In 1971, the Ocean Steamship Company and the Inchcape Group formed Ocean Inchcape with Ocean owning a 60 per cent share in the venture. The group's name was changed to the Ocean Transport & Trading Company Limited in 1972, and it was divided into six divisions: Liner Shipping, Specialised Shipping, Ship Procurement, Ship Management, Distribution, and South-East Asia. Holt's Wharf in Hong Kong was sold in 1971. OCL was taken over by P&O in 1986, and a decision was made to build several bulk carriers and tankers in 1971-75, as part of a diversification policy, when it became clear that the traditional cargo trade was in decline. MSAS Cargo International, which was formed in 1968 as McGregor Swire Air Services, was acquired as a joint venture. The holding in the Straits Steamship Company was increased from 35.2 per cent to 64.4 per cent in 1973.

William Cory & Son was acquired by the Ocean Group in 1972 and the Barber Blue Sea Line was formed in 1974 as a merger between Barber Lines and Blue Sea Line and the group's 50 per cent share in the China Navigation Company was sold to John Swire in 1976. Glen Line and Nederlandsche Stoomvaart Maatschappij 'Oceaan' were merged with Ben Line, forming the Ben Ocean Service. The Dutch Line lasted until 1978, when it ceased trading. The P-class ships were sold at the end of the 1970s, and *Centaur* (3) was chartered to Curnow's St Helena Shipping Company and replaced by *Berlin*, which was renamed *Princess Mahsuri*.

In the 1970s, the company had four container ships, *Menelaus*, *Memnon*, *Menetheus* and *Melampus*, built in Japanese yards, and went back to Scott's at Greenock for the last class of vessels to be built for them. *Maron*, *Mentor* and *Myrmidon* had a very short life with the Ocean Group and were sold for further trading before the end of the 1980s. A significant decision was made in 1980 to move the headquarters of the company from India Buildings in Liverpool to London. The company's training facilities in Liverpool were reorganised in 1981 and were finally closed at the end of 1986. The shareholding in the Straits Steamship Company was sold in 1983. Palm Line, owned by Unilever, was bought in 1984. *Barber Perseus* and *Barber Hector* were built as the Ocean Group's contribution towards the Barber Blue Sea consortium, which they withdrew from in 1988.

Ocean's share in the Overseas Container Line was sold to P&O in 1986, who transferred their holding in Panocean Storage & Transport and the remaining vessels in the deep-sea fleet were transferred to the Isle of Man register the following year. In October 1984, changes were announced for the Marine Division of Ocean Transport & Trading, to include replacement of Ocean Liners Limited and Ocean Fleets Limited by Ocean Marine within the head office. Mr N. C. F. Barber, division managing director, said that this would not affect the external use of the name Ocean Fleets Limited. An unsuccessful takeover bid was made in 1986 by a New Zealand entrepreneur, and India Buildings in Liverpool was sold in 1988. Nicholas Barber, who joined the company in 1964, was appointed Chief Executive in 1987. The Elder Dempster Line, Palm Line and the Guinea Gulf Lines were sold to the French company Société Navale Chargeurs Delmas-Vieljeux (SNCDV) in 1989.

When *Memnon* arrived at Falmouth in April 1989 for inspection prior to sale to the Pacific International Line, the Ocean Transport & Trading Company moved out of deep-sea trading to concentrate in offshore operations. In the early 1990s, the group's main business was in international freight management and MSAS Cargo International was one of the world's leading freight forwarders with over 220 offices in thirty countries. By 1996, Cory Towage had a fleet of fifty-six tugs operating in fourteen ports in the United Kingdom, Ireland and Canada and, under contract, in Angola and Panama. The offshore business had an established presence in the North Sea, West Africa, South-East Asia, Brazil, India and the Middle East. The distribution sector included McGregor Cory and Panocean Storage & Transport which specialised in moving and storing bulk liquids in Europe and the United States. The marine sector included OIL Limited, which provided support services for the offshore oil industry worldwide.

The group reported a pre-tax profit of £83.1 million in 1998, which was up by 13 per cent on the 1997 profit of £73.5 million. New contracts were gained in Oman and Venezuela, but progress in the United Kingdom business was only satisfactory in overall terms. MSAS Global Logistics was created, which combined all of its logistic business, including MSAS Cargo International, under the new name. Joint ventures in China and subsidiaries in Finland and Korea were established and Intexo and Marken were purchased. In 1998, they took over Oslo Havnelager, Mercury, Laker Cargo, Skyking, A. W. Fenton and Dutch Air. Mark VII, Malenstein, Parkhill Reclamation and Aerocar Spedition AB were acquired in 1999.

Consequently, it came as no surprise that the group had finally withdrawn from owning ships early in 2000. It sold Cory Towage to the Dutch company Wijsmuller for £81.8 million. Ocean said that the sale would enable it to develop the logistics and waste management activities of Cory Environment, which operated landfill disposal of waste and municipal services, such as refuse collection and street cleaning. Ocean Group plc and the National Freight Corporation merged in 2000 to form Exel plc, creating the world's second-largest logistic group. It brought together Ocean Group's strengths in transporting goods internationally by air and sea freight with NFL's expertise in handling supply chains on the ground. The groups had complementary customer bases, with Ocean being strong in healthcare and technology and NFL in automotive, chemical and retail sectors. The chief executive of the Ocean Group, John Allan, said that Exel would be able to manage entire chains from raw material sourcing to delivery to the customer. Gerry Murphy, chief executive of the National Freight Corporation, described it as a merger of equals and predicted it would generate £15 million of savings within two years.

The new company would handle logistics for around 70 per cent of the world's top 250 companies. The company was debt-free and planned to expand its sea-freight operations. NFL's John Devaney and David Finch became chairman and chief financial officer of Exel, and Ocean's chairman, Nigel Rich, became deputy chairman. Exel plc acquired Tibbett & Britten, a leading British contract logistics business, and Deutsche Post took over Exel in December 2005. On completion of the deal, Deutsche Post added DHL Express to operate as DHL Exel Supply Chain.

THE SHIPS

Name **Year** **GRT** **Dimensions** **Engines** **Net Tons** **Speed**

Dumbarton Youth 1847 239 126x21.9x12.8 Steam Expansion 187 8 knots
B William Denny & Brothers, Dumbarton.
She was ordered as a collier by Mr Whyte with her sister *Mazeppa* and both were owned by Henry Smith. In 1852, she was sold to Thomas Ainsworth and George Holt, and Alfred Holt was the agent and supervising engineer. She was employed on the Whitehaven to Cardiff service and later from Liverpool to Bordeaux.

Cleator 1854 391 183.9x24.3x14.3 Steam Expansion 341 8 knots
B Cato & Miller, Brunswick Dock, Liverpool.
Owned by Alfred and Philip Holt and purchased with money from the Ainsworth family of Cleator. In 1855, she was chartered by the French Government during the Crimean War and was later employed in the Mediterranean to Istanbul, or the Crimea. She was fitted with Alfred Holt's compound tandem engine in 1864, which produced steam pressure that was three times that of other vessels. She was lengthened in 1869 and sailed through the Suez Canal. Sold to J. D. Ross three years later, and renamed *Alastor*, sailing from Labuan.

Saladin 1855 535 183.9x24.3x14.3 Steam Expansion — 8 knots
B Cato & Miller, Brunswick Dock, Liverpool.
It was planned to place her on charter, but when the Crimean War ended, she was employed on the Liverpool to West Indies service. The project proved very successful for Alfred Holt, who was spending more time managing his shipping interests. *Saladin* was sold to the West India & Pacific Steamship Company and later to Lamport & Holt in 1864. Purchased by J. Martin & Company in 1872, G. Moller & Company of Konigsberg, Germany, in 1877, T. H. Bahring, Konigsberg, in 1881, and Storrer & Scott, Konigsberg, the following year. She was re-engined, became *Samland*, and was wrecked on Oesel Island on 22 May 1907.

Plantagenet 1859 695 202.0x24.3x14.3 Steam Expansion — 9 knots
B Scott & Company, Greenock.
She was employed on the service to the West Indies until she was sold to the West India & Pacific Steamship Company in 1864. She was wrecked near Brest on 14 September 1869 on a voyage from Malta to Liverpool.

Askalon 1861 975 228.0x24.3x14.3 Steam Expansion — —
B Scott & Company, Greenock.
Launched on 7 October 1861 and employed on the West Indies service. Sold to the West India & Pacific Steamship Company in 1864 and abandoned on 15 January the following year in the North Atlantic.

Talisman 1860 738 202.0x24.3x14.3 Steam Expansion — 9 knots
B Scott & Company, Greenock.
Launched on 3 November 1860 and employed on the West Indies service. She was sold to the West India & Pacific Steamship Company in 1864 and to Lamport & Holt the following year. On 21 January 1873, she sank near the Burlings, Portugal, on a voyage from Santos to Hamburg.

Crusader 1862 901 221.3x30.4x17.7 Steam Expansion — 8½ knots
B Scott & Company, Greenock.
Entered service on the West Indies route in 1862 and was sold to the West India & Pacific Steamship Company two years later. She was wrecked on Galera Zambra Island, near Cartagena, Colombia, on 4 January 1871.

Agamemnon.

Achilles.

Agamemnon 1865 2,280 309.5x38.8x28.4 Compound Tandem Steam 1,550 10 knots
B Scott & Company, Greenock, and designed by Alfred Holt.
The three-ship order cost the company £156,000 and *Agamemnon* sailed on her maiden voyage from Liverpool to Mauritius, Penang, Singapore, Hong Kong and Shanghai on 19 April 1866. The vessel took seventy-seven days on the return voyage with additional calls, including Foochow. In 1869, she loaded 2,516,000 lb of tea crop at Hankow, which was the largest loaded in a ship with a record freight rate of £28,087. She was transferred to Nederlandsche Stoomvaart Maatschappij 'Oceaan' in 1897 and was broken up in Italy two years later.

Ajax 1865 2,280 309.5x38.8x28.4 Compound Tandem Steam 1,550 10 knots
B Scott & Company, Greenock.
She was the second sister of the three-ship order and sailed on her maiden voyage in 1866. She sank at Shanghai in 1868 when the propeller shaft had been disconnected for the engineer to service the parts and carry out engine-running tests. As the tide went out, the shaft unscrewed, allowing water to enter the vessel, with the superstructure above the water level. Alfred Holt accepted this as a design fault and watertight glands were fitted in the shaft tunnels of all Holt ships. *Ajax* was also transferred to NSM 'Oceaan' in 1897, and in 1900, it was planned to reboiler her, but when this was found not be economical, she was scrapped at Genoa.

Achilles 1866 2,280 309.5x38.8x28.4 Compound Tandem Steam 1,550 10 knots
B Scott & Company, Greenock.
She cost £45,500 to build, and on arrival at Shanghai in 1866, she found that there was no cargo for her return journey. The newly formed company, Butterfield & Swire, offered a part cargo of shirtings for Lancashire, and the voyage became profitable. This impressed Alfred Holt, and the firm were appointed as agents in Shanghai. He also recognised that the firm were involved in textiles and silks in addition to tea and the two firms began a long and profitable relationship, which lasted many years.

In November 1869, on her homeward voyage, *Achilles* became the first of the company's vessels to use the Suez Canal. Between 1876 and 1878, the machinery on Holt's earlier ships was replaced by new engines, which increased their performance. *Achilles* was transferred to NSM 'Oceaan' in 1891 and was broken up at Genoa in 1898.

Diomed 1868 1,848 291.5x34.5x28.3 Compound Tandem Steam 1,201 10 knots
She was the first of a class of seven ships and was originally ordered from Scott & Company, who went into temporary bankruptcy in 1867. The order was transferred to Andrew Leslie & Company at Newcastle and the hull was redesigned with a wider beam. One of the reasons for this was that Alfred Holt recognised that the original trio had been overpowered for the route and the compound engine was also reduced by 20 per cent.

Diomed entered service in 1868 and was sold to Yamamoto Tosuke of Osaka, Japan, and renamed *Genzan Maru* in 1894. She was wrecked on 8 October 1903 at Nemouro on the western tip of Hokkaido.

Nestor 1868 1,869 313.6x32.8x27.9 Compound Tandem Steam 1,414 10 knots
B Andrew Leslie & Company, Hebburn on Tyne.
She entered service in 1868 and was sold to Japanese owners in 1894, becoming *Daisan Mayoshima Maru* and *Mayayoshi Maru* No. 3 when she was sold again to Fukunaga Shoshiki, Kobe. On 9 November that year, she was transporting troops during the Russo-Japanese War and was lost at Si-yuen-chang.

Priam 1870 2,039 313.6x32.8x27.9 Compound Tandem Steam 1,572 10 knots
B Scott & Company, Greenock.
She entered service in 1870 and was wrecked off Sisgarsas Island, near Corunna, Spain, on 11 January 1889 on a voyage from Liverpool to Hong Kong.

Sarpedon 1871 1,949 310.7x33.5x25.5 Compound Tandem Steam 1,519 10 knots
B Andrew Leslie & Company, Hebburn on Tyne.
Handed over to the company in 1871, for the services to the Far East. On 4 September 1876, on a voyage from Shanghai to London, she sank off Ushant following a collision with the Belgian vessel *Julia David*, which was owned by David Verberst & Company of Antwerp. A long court case followed which initially found in favour of the Belgian line. However, a steward named Mayer said that the witnesses had committed perjury and the verdict was overturned.

Hector 1871 1,956 312.1x34.5x28.3 Compound Tandem Steam 1,523 10 knots
B Andrew Leslie & Company, Hebburn on Tyne.
Entered service in 1871 but was lost when she ran aground outside Amoy harbour, close to Xiamen on a voyage from Shanghai on 4 October 1875. This was their first total loss.

Ulysses 1871 1,949 291.5x34.5x28.3 Compound Tandem Steam 1,519 10 knots
B Andrew Leslie & Company, Hebburn on Tyne.
On her maiden voyage in 1871, she grounded in the Red Sea and had to return to Liverpool. The following year, she shed her propeller as she entered Shanghai and drifted ashore without any serious damage or injury. On 16 August 1887, she also ran aground on Jubal Island in the Gulf of Suez on a voyage from London to Penang. Later that year, she was written off as a total loss.

Menelaus 1871 1,956 312.2x34.5x28.3 Compound Tandem Steam 1,523 10 knots
B Andrew Leslie & Company, Hebburn on Tyne.
The last of the five *Diomed* class. She was transferred to NSM 'Oceaan' in 1891 and was broken up at Briton Ferry in 1894.

Patroclus 1872 2,074 328.6x32.6x25.3 Compound Tandem Steam 1,604 10 knots
B Andrew Leslie & Company, Hebburn on Tyne.
Patroclus was the lead vessel of the four vessels that also included *Glaucus*, *Deucalion* and *Antenor*, but was the second ship to enter service. She was also the first vessel of eighteen similar vessels built for the company. She was reboilered after ten years of service, transferred to NSM 'Oceaan' in 1892 and sold to Minamishima Masuku, Tokyo, in 1895 and renamed *Shiganoura Maru*. Sold to Nagata Sanjuro later that year and broken up in Japan in 1924.

Glaucus 1871 2,074 328.6x32.6x25.3 Compound Tandem Steam 1,604 10 knots
B Andrew Leslie & Company, Hebburn on Tyne.
Transferred to NSM 'Oceaan' in 1891. Sold to Japanese interests in 1898, renamed *Jintsu Maru* and was wrecked at Shimoda, near Nagoya on Honshu, on 28 June that year.

Deucalion 1872 2,074 328.6x32.6x25.3 Compound Tandem Steam 1,604 10 knots
B Andrew Leslie & Company, Hebburn on Tyne.
She remained in the fleet until 1891, when she was transferred to NSM 'Oceaan'. In 1896, she retained her name when she was transferred to the subsidiary company, East Indian Ocean Steamship Company, which was bought by Norddeutscher Lloyd and managed by A. O. Mayer in 1899. *Deucalion* was registered as owned by Bremen Lloyd and became *Sandaken*.

Became *Tai Ping* when she was acquired by Tung Kee & Company of Shanghai in 1903 and was taken over by the Russian interests in 1907 after the Sino-Japanese war. She was renamed *Ermack* by Ellwanger Brothers of Vladivostok, and was owned by Kusnetsov Brothers, also of Vladivostok, in 1911 and was broken up at Shanghai two years later.

Antenor 1872 2,162 328.6x32.6x25.3 Compound Tandem Steam 1,241 10 knots
B Andrew Leslie & Company, Hebburn on Tyne.
Antenor was also reboilered in 1884 and was transferred to NSM 'Oceaan' in 1891. Two years later, she was sold to Baba Dokiu, Tokyo, renamed *Tateyama Maru* and owned by Baba Michihisa, Higashi, Iwase, later that year. In 1921, she was sold to Inukami Keigoro of Nishinomaya and was broken up in Japan in 1929 after fifty-seven years service.

Stentor 1875 2,025 314.1x35.2x26.0 Compound Tandem Steam 1,278 10 knots
B Scott & Company, Greenock.
Sailed for the Blue Funnel Line until 1891, when she was transferred to NSM 'Oceaan'. In 1896, she was sold to E. Nathan at Singapore, renamed *Charterhouse*, and to Lin Ho Puah of Singapore in 1900. On 30 September 1906, she sank during a typhoon off Hai-Nan on a voyage from Haihow to Hong Kong, when all on board were lost.

Anchises 1875 2,021 314.1x35.2x26.0 Compound Tandem Steam 1,304 10 knots
B Scott & Company, Greenock.
Completed with a single square-rigged sail on the foremast and transferred to NSM 'Oceaan' in 1891 and back to the British register in 1895. The following year, she was sold to Ung Lee Koo of Penang, retaining the British flag. On 26 June that year, she was wrecked near Rangoon on a voyage to Singapore.

Orestes 1875 2,057 316.5x35.2x26.0 Compound Tandem Steam 1,323 10 knots
B Scott & Company, Greenock.
She had a very short life, as she was lost off Galle, Sri Lanka, on a voyage from Liverpool to Penang on 7 March 1876.

Orestes (2) 1877 2,057 316.5x35.2x26.0 Compound Tandem Steam 1,323 10 knots
B Scott & Company, Greenock.
Built as a replacement for Orestes (1) and when she was sold to Japanese interests in 1894 she was wrecked on the delivery voyage bearing the name Orestes.

Teucer 1877 2,057 316.5x35.2x26.0 Compound Tandem Steam 1,303 10 knots
B Scott & Company, Greenock.
On completion, she was the first steel-hulled vessel owned by the company and was wrecked off Ushant on 30 May 1885 on a voyage from Singapore to Amsterdam.

Sarpedon (2) 1877 2,036 310.0x34.2x25.3 Compound Tandem Steam 1,592 10 knots
B Andrew Leslie & Company, Hebburn on Tyne.
In 1893, she was transferred to NSM 'Oceaan' and was sold to Gomei Kwaisha Umenura Tasaka Kwaisoten, Tokyo, in 1894, becoming *Tamahime Maru*. She was wrecked off the coast of Japan on 4 October 1896.

Hector (2) 1877 2,111 316.8x33.5x24.7 Compound Tandem Steam 1,570 10 knots
B Andrew Leslie & Company, Hebburn on Tyne.
Transferred to NSM 'Oceaan' in 1891 and was renamed *Moji Maru* when she was owned by Nippon Yusen KK in 1894. Sold to Kamiya Dembei, Yokohama, in 1910, Gomei Kaisha ida Shoten in 1918, Mojimaru Goshi Kaisya of Kobe in 1924, and was broken up in Fuchu, Japan, in 1930.

Ganymede 1879 405 166.5x28.0x10.8 — 236 8 knots
B Scott & Company, Greenock.
Ganymede was ordered for the Sumatra to Singapore tobacco trade and cost £11,000 to build and ran between Belawan Deli and Singapore. She was transferred to NSM 'Oceaan' in 1894 and sold in 1900.

Sarah Nicholson 1865 934 194.7x32.7x22.6 Iron sailing ship — —
B Nicholson & Company, Annan.
She was built as a sailing barque for Nicholson & Company of Dumfries and purchased by Alfred Holt in 1880 and converted to a hulk for the storage of tobacco at Singapore. She arrived at Deli by tow and was used there until a dedicated storage warehouse was built the following year.

Laertes 1879 2,097 320.5x34.3x26.0 Compound Tandem Steam 1,482 10 knots
B Scott & Company, Greenock.
The first ship of a class of ten vessels with smaller powered engines and an improved hull design and a larger cargo capacity. She was transferred to NSM 'Oceaan' in 1894 and back to the Ocean Steamship Company in 1901. Purchased by Li Shek Pang of Hong Kong in 1903, retaining the same name as when owned by Hung Hing Steamship Company. Sank following a collision in the Malacca Strait on 15 December 1917 while sailing in ballast from Rangoon to Singapore.

Cyclops 1880 2,064 321.4x34.3x26.0 Compound Tandem Steam 1,499 10 knots
B Scott & Company, Greenock.
She was handed over to the company in April 1880 and operated on their routes until 1894, when she was transferred to NSM 'Oceaan'. Bought by R. Rup and Giulfo of Montevideo in 1902, renamed *Iberia*, and was broken up at Montevideo two years later.

Bellerophon 1880 2,154 320.0x34.3x26.0 Compound Tandem Steam 1,318 10 knots
B Scott & Company, Greenock.
Sister of *Laertes* and was transferred to NSM 'Oceaan' in 1893. She was sold to Manakani Toshiro Uraga five years later, and became *Nitto Maru* in 1900, when she was sold to T. Okasaki of Kobe, Japan. On 4 April 1915, she was wrecked at Tamagawa on a voyage from Otaru to Nagoya.

Telemachus 1880 2,186 320.9x34.3x26.0 Compound Tandem Steam 1,340 10 knots
B Andrew Leslie & Company, Hebburn on Tyne.
Sister of *Laertes*, transferred to NSM 'Oceaan' in 1894 and back to the Ocean Steamship Company in 1899. She was sold three years later to Li Shek Pang, Hong Kong, who also purchased the *Laertes* and both retained their original names. *Telemachus* remained in service with them until she was sold and broken up at Hong Kong in 1936.

Jason 1880 2,187 320.5x34.3x26.0 Compound Tandem Steam 1,336 10 knots
B Andrew Leslie & Company, Hebburn on Tyne.
After fourteen years of service, she was transferred to NSM 'Oceaan' in 1894 and renamed *Ugo Maru* in 1903, when she was sold to Akita Kisen KK, Hakodate. Bought by Okazaki KKK of Kobe in 1913, owned by Mitsubayashi Naosuke, Amagasaki, and renamed *Nichiun Maru* in 1920 and broken up in Japan two years later.

Palamed 1885 2,479 320.2x36.3x25.9 Compound Tandem Steam 1,537 10 knots
B Andrew Leslie, Newcastle.
Renamed *Kwan-On Maru* No. 15 in 1897, when she was sold to Oakai Kikusaburo of Kobe, and on resale to Busai Kisen KK in 1913, she became *Nichinan Maru*. She was wrecked off the coast of Korea on 5 January 1928.

Palinurus 1886 2,523 320.2x36.3x25.9 Compound Tandem Steam 1,564 10 knots
B Hawthorn, Leslie & Company, Newcastle.
Transferred to NSM 'Oceaan' in 1896, and returned to the British flag the following year. Sold to Oakai Kikusaburo, Kobe, later that year and renamed *Kwan-On Maru* No. 20. Sold to Okazaki KKK of Kobe in 1913, becoming *Nippoku Maru*, purchased by Goho Shokai KK, Susami, in 1920, Seito Kaiun KK, Nishinomiya, in 1923, and broken up in Japan later that year.

Prometheus 1886 2,376 320.2x36.3x25.9 Compound Tandem Steam 1,554 10 knots
B Scott & Company, Greenock.
In 1894, she was transferred to NSM 'Oceaan' and then sold to Nippon Yusen Kaisha, Tokyo, and renamed *Ushina Maru*. Her name was later changed to *Ujina Maru* when she was taken over by the Japanese Government and used as a troopship in the Russo-Japanese War that year. However, on 10 May the following year, she was wrecked on the east coast of Japan in the Gulf of Tai Lin Wau.

Dardanus 1886 2,502 320.2x36.3x25.9 Compound Tandem Steam 1,551 10 knots
B Hawthorn, Leslie & Company, Newcastle.
Sold to Nippon Yusen Kabusiki Kaisya of Tokyo in 1894 and was sunk as a block ship at Port Arthur on 3 May 1903.

Ulysses (2) 1886 2,140 320.8x36.3x25.8 Triple Expansion 1,372 10 knots
B Scott & Company, Greenock.
She was the first triple-expansion ship in the fleet, but the company soon reverted back to compound tandem. On a voyage from Shanghai to Yokohama, she was wrecked near Tanabe, Japan, on 21 April 1890.

Ascanius 1880 107 74.0x18.1x7.5 — 74 9 knots
B Cochrane & Company, Birkenhead.
Iron tug built for towing duties at Singapore. Towed *Sarah Nicholson* to Deli in 1880 and sold to Ah Hi of Saigon in 1890 and broken up in 1914.

Andes 1859 328 — Sailing barque — —
B Williamson & Company.
Purchased in 1880 and used as a storage hulk for tobacco at Penang.

Fantee 1879 167 120.2x18.0x8.4 — — 9 knots
B Alexander Stephen & Sons, Linthouse.
She was built for service at Singapore and was used with a metal smelter in 1890 and sold to W. Kinsey in 1894 for use as a hulk for storage of goods. Broken up in 1900.

Mercury 1892 303 138.6x21.7x12.0 — 189 9 knots
B J.Taylor & Company, Birkenhead.
She was built for the Oceanic Steamship Company in 1872 and purchased by Alfred Holt in 1881 for use as a tobacco vessel in Singapore. In 1900, she was sold to Tanjong Pagar Dock Company of Singapore for use as a storage ship at that port.

Memnon 1861 1,290 253.6x32.6x23.0 — — —
B Scott & Company, Greenock.
She was built for Lamport & Holt Line for their services to Brazil and River Plate services and was re-engined in 1872. Purchased by the Ocean Steamship Company in 1883 and re-boilered five years later. In 1893, she was transferred to the East India Ocean Steamship Company with Alfred Holt as owner, becoming a hulk in Singapore in 1899.

Hebe 1885 545 190.0x30.7x11.6 — — 9 knots
B Scott & Company, Greenock.

In 1910, she was sold to C. Willis & Partners of Singapore as a tobacco carrier, bought by the Straits Steamship Company in 1912 and broken up ten years later.

Calypso 1889 544 190.0x30.7x11.6 — — —
B Scott & Company, Greenock.
Sister of *Hebe*. Purchased by the Straits Steamship Company in 1912 and broken up at Singapore in 1929.

Sappho 1887 532 190.0x30.7x11.6 — — —
B Scott & Company, Greenock.
Sister of *Hebe*. She was sold to the Straits Steamship Company in 1890, and it was claimed that she was part funded by Theodore Bogaardt. In 1899, she went aground at Palau Oudon and was refloated. Sold to the Menam Pilot's Association, Bangkok, in 1923 and used as a pilot station and was broken up in 1928.

Telamon 1885 2,292 320.0x36.3x25.8 Compound Tandem Steam 1,632 10 knots
B Scott & Company, Greenock.
Transferred to NSM 'Oceaan' in 1897 and was broken up at Genoa in 1902.

Titan 1885 2,283 320.2x36.3x25.9 Compound Tandem Steam 1,621 10 knots
B Scott & Company, Greenock.
Transferred to NSM 'Oceaan' in 1895 and broken up at Genoa in 1902.

Hecuba 1882 918 233.4x32.6x15.8 — 590 10 knots
B Scott & Company, Greenock.
Designed and built for the Bangkok to Singapore rice trade and was owned by the Ocean Steamship Company, Mansfield and Bogaardt, managed by the East India Ocean Steamship Company. She was sold to Norddeutscher Lloyd in 1899, becoming *Kadut* and *Matsushima Maru* in 1905, when purchased by Hokuriku Kisen Goshi Kaisya of Osaka.

Medusa 1885 967 237.4x34.2x15.4 — — 9 knots
B W. H. Potter & Sons, Queens Dock, Liverpool.
She was owned by the Ocean Steamship Company, Bogaardt, Mansfield and Crompton, managed by the East India Steamship Company. Purchased by Norddeutscher Lloyd in 1899 and renamed *Kelantan*. Sold to Y. Kaji of Kobe in 1903 and renamed *Jingi Maru* No. 3, later to Y. Fujiyama, and broken up in 1921.

Hecate 1885 968 237.4x34.2x15.4 — 609 9 knots
B W. H. Potter & Sons, Queens Dock, Liverpool.
Sister of *Medusa*. Built for the Bangkok to Singapore tobacco service with the same ownership and managed by the East India Ocean Steamship Company. Renamed *Patani* when purchased by Norddeutscher Lloyd in 1899, *Ikuta Maru* No.2 in 1904 and *Hokuyo Maru* in 1908 when owned by Hokuyo Kisen KK and later owned by Yamamoto Atuzo. She was broken up in 1924.

Hydra 1889 990 237.3x34.2x15.4 — 619 9 knots
B W. H. Potter & Sons, Queens Dock, Liverpool.
Sister of *Medusa*. Designed for the Swatow to Singapore and Bangkok service with the same joint ownership, managed by the East India Ocean Steamship Company. Sold to Norddeutscher Lloyd in 1899, becoming *Kedah* and *Sekkai Maru* in 1905, when owned by Y. Fujiyama, Nishinomiya. She was broken up in 1918.

Will o' the Wisp 1883 283 120.4x22.2x10.0 — — 8 knots
B Norfolk & Company, Hull.
She was built for W. S. Davison and was sold to Walter Mansfield & Company of Singapore, and A. P. Adams was registered as the owner. Sold to Alfred Holt in 1887 and transferred to the Straits Steamship Company in 1890. Purchased by Tan Poh Tong of Singapore in 1896, Tan Hok Hay in 1898, Lim Kee Joo in 1899, Ng Nguan Teng in 1900, Sug Toon Ghee in 1906, K. A. Somasuntheran Chitty in 1908, Wee Brothers Steamship Company in 1909, Wong Poh Keung and H. A. Lamont in 1917, Wee Seng Bee Steamship Company and A. L. Alves in 1918, Wee Teow Beng in 1923, Teo Hu Lai in 1924, the Heap Engineering Moh. Steamship Company in 1935 and was broken up later that year.

Flintshire 1872 1,565 270.7x32.8x28.8 — — 9 knots
B London & Glasgow Company, Glasgow.
Built for Jenkin's Shire Line. She was reboilered in 1882 and sold to Lim Tiang Hee of Singapore in 1888. Purchased by the Ocean Steamship Company the following year and based at Singapore. Transferred to the East India Ocean Steamship Company in 1891 and to NSM 'Oceaan' the following year and back to the East India Company in 1895. She was sold to Okazaki Tokichi of Kobe in 1896, becoming *Yayeyama Maru*. On 12 December 1898, she was involved in a collision and sank at Nagasaki.

Saladin 1890 1,874 254.6x38.2x24.0 — — 10 knots
B Thomas Royden & Company, Liverpool.
She was designed for the Singapore to Batavia and Fremantle service, owned by

Alfred Holt and operated with the West Australian Steam Navigation Company. In 1905, she was sold to *Kawasaki Yoshitaro* of Kobe, becoming *Kotohira Maru* No. 3, and then to Kentaro Kawachi. She was broken up in 1926.

Myrmidon 1890 2,868 336.1x38.5x27.0 Compound Tandem Steam 1,591 10 knots
B Scott & Company, Greenock.
The first of a class of four ships, which cost £52,320 and carried twelve passengers in cabins, 500 deck pilgrims and 200 'tween deck passengers. Transferred to NSM 'Oceaan' in 1899 and sold to Tatsuma Shokwi KK, Naruo, in 1904 and renamed *Tatsu Maru*. Purchased by Tatsuma Kisen KK, Nishinomaya, in 1911, becoming *Tencho Maru*, *Hai Tien*, under the Chinese flag in 1920, and *Ho Ping*, owned by Tsieging Chin of Chefoo in 1927. She was broken up at Hong Kong two years later.

Teucer (2) 1890 2,846 336.1x38.5x27.0 Compound Tandem Steam 1,741 10 knots
B Scott & Company, Greenock.
Sister of *Myrmidon*. Transferred to NSM 'Oceaan' in 1890, and back under the British flag in 1903. Sold to K. Matsugata of Kobe and renamed *Chusa Maru* in 1906. Wrecked near to Toto, Japan, on 9 August 1907.

Polyphemus 1890 2,868 336.1x38.5x27.0 Compound Tandem Steam 1,816 10 knots
Sister of *Myrmidon* and was able to undertake Mecca pilgrimage voyages from Singapore. Transferred to NSM 'Oceaan' in 1898 and sold to Tatsuma Shokwi KK, Naruo, in 1904, becoming *Tatsu Maru* No. 2. She was renamed *Chikyu Maru* in 1911 and was wrecked off the coast of Korea at Joshin on 31 January 1916.

Teucer (2).

Priam (2) 1890 2,868 336.1x38.5x27.0 Compound Tandem Steam 1,816 10 knots
B Scott & Company, Greenock.
Sister of *Myrmidon*. Transferred to NSM 'Oceaan' in 1899 and sold to K. Kishimoto, Hamadera, in 1903 and renamed *Shingu Maru*. Sold to Nippon Kosen Gyogyo KK, Foetsyo, in 1914. She became the *Singu Maru* in 1938, owned by Nippon Suisan KK and was owned by Sansin Kisen KK, Hutyo, in 1942. She was bombed and sunk by an American air attack south-west of Formosa on 3 May 1944.

Ixion 1892 3,627 354.9x42.8x26.7 Triple Expansion 2,286 10 knots
B Scott & Company, Greenock.
First ship in a class of four vessels, and the first of a new design of three island superstructure. After ten years service, she was transferred to NSM 'Oceaan' in 1902 and was lost off Enggano, Indonesia, when she suffered a serious fire on a voyage from Java to Amsterdam on 2 October 1911.

Tantalus 1892 3,627 354.9x42.8x26.7 Triple Expansion 2,286 10 knots
B Scott & Company, Greenock.
Ixion class. Transferred to NSM 'Oceaan' in 1904 and became *Florian Geyer* in 1922, when she was sold to Leonard R. Muller at Hamburg. She was broken up there two years later.

Ulysses (3) 1892 3,261 354.9x42.8x26.7 Triple Expansion 2,286 10 knots
B Scott & Company, Greenock.
Ixion class. Sold to Japanese interests in 1912, renamed *Daisai Maru*, and following the First World War, she was transferred to the French Government and became St Medard, renamed General Moiner in 1920, St Medard again in 1921, owned by Société Maritime Française, La Rochelle. She was broken up at Ardrossan in 1924.

Pyrrhus 1892 3,627 354.9x42.8x26.7 Triple Expansion 2,286 10 knots
B Scott & Company, Greenock.
Ixion class. Transferred to NSM 'Oceaan' in 1907 and sold to Japan in 1914, when she was renamed *Shingo Maru*. In 1916, she was sold to Madrigal & Company, Manila and became Macaria. In 1917, she was taken over by the United States as a transport and renamed *Villemer*. On 7 November that year, she was torpedoed by UC-38 east of Crete.

Beagle 1892 147 110.5x20.2x6.9 100 — — 8 knots
B Blackwood & Gordon, Port Glasgow.

She was a steam lighter based at Cossack, Western Australia, and was sold to Italian interests in 1908 and to the Government of Siam the following year.

Nestor (2) 1889 3,767 370.5x42.2x27.2 Triple Expansion 2,417 10 knots
B Schlesinger, Davies & Company, Newcastle.
Built as *Sullamut* for Hajee Jasoob Poorbhoy, Bombay, and was renamed *Queen of India* by Beyts, Craig & Company. Purchased by Ocean Steamship Company in 1894, renamed *Nestor* and refurbished at a cost of £37,000. Sold in 1911 to an Italian company, who renamed her *Teresa*, and later *Assunzione*. On 15 June 1917, she was torpedoed and sunk in the Mediterranean.

Cerberus 1894 1,754 257.3x41.1x20.9 Triple Expansion 1,123 10 knots
B Workman, Clark & Company, Belfast.
Built for Alfred Holt and operated by the East India Steamship Company. Sold to Norddeutscher Lloyd, Bremen, in 1899 and renamed *Singora*. In 1910, she was purchased by Y. Hachiuma, Nishinomayam and renamed *Tamon Maru* No. 1. Sold to Shizaki Yokichi, Kobe, in 1925 and broken up in Japan in 1931.

Sultan 1894 2,063 258.5x11.6x13.9 Triple Expansion 1,270 10 knots
B Workman, Clark & Company, Belfast.
Owned by the Ocean Steamship Company, and the West Australian Steam Navigation on a joint basis for operation on the Singapore to Batavia and Fremantle service. In 1898, she became wholly owned by Alfred Holt and was sold to Oaki Goshi Kaisya of Yokohama in 1909, becoming *Kayo Maru*. After being laid up at Yokohama, she was finally broken up there in 1931.

Orestes (3) 1894 4,653 392.3x47.1x26.4 Triple Expansion 2,992 10 knots
B Scott & Company, Greenock.
Lead ship for a class of six vessels. In 1901, she opened the Liverpool to Australia service for the company and survived until 1925, when she was sold to be broken up in Italy.

Sarpedon (3) 1894 4,663 391.5 x47.1x26.4 Triple Expansion 3,023 10 knots
B Workman, Clark & Company, Belfast.
Orestes class. Transferred to KSM 'Oceaan' in 1914, returning to British register the following year to replace tonnage lost by enemy action. She survived a torpedo attack in the Mediterranean on 7 November 1918, which was the final German action on a Blue Funnel vessel in the First World War. In 1923, she was sold to Leonard R. Muller of Hamburg, renamed *Gotz von Berlichingen* and broken up there two years later.

Dardanus (2) 1894 4,653 392.3x47.1x26.4 Triple Expansion 2,992 10 knots
B Scott & Company, Greenock.
Orestes class. Transferred to NSM 'Oceaan' in 1911 and sold to Paulsen & Ivers of Kiel in 1923, becoming *Fingal*. Renamed *Fortunato Secondo* when acquired by INSA of Genoa in 1926 and was broken up there the following year.

Diomed (2) 1895 4,653 392.0x47.1x26.4 Triple Expansion 3,005 10 knots
B Scott & Company, Greenock.
Orestes class. On 22 August 1915, she was torpedoed and sank 57 miles off the Scilly Isles. The captain and two other members of her crew were killed on the bridge.

Hector (3) 1895 4,653 391.5x47.1x26.4 Triple Expansion 3,006 10 knots
B Workman, Clark & Company, Belfast.
Orestes class. In 1915, she served as a balloon ship during the Dardanelles campaign and was sold for demolition at Wilhelmshaven in 1923.

Menelaus (2) 1895 4,653 392.3x47.1x26.4 Triple Expansion 3,006 10 knots
B Scott & Company, Greenock.
Orestes class. In 1916, she was acquired by the Admiralty, renamed *Davo* and used as a balloon ship. She was broken up at Genoa in 1923.

Centaur 1895 1,900 278.Ox41.1x20.8 Triple Expansion 1,223 10 knots
B Workman, Clark & Company, Belfast.
She was designed and built for the East India Steamship Company and was sold to Norddeutscher Lloyd in 1899 and renamed *Korat*. In 1911, she was sold to Japanese interests, becoming *Daito Maru*, and survived until 1918.

Prometheus (2) 1896 5,570 422.0x49.0x38.3 Triple Expansion 3,583 10 knots
B Scott & Company, Greenock.
Lead ship of a class of four vessels. After twenty-eight years service, she was sold to INSA of Genoa in 1924, renamed *Delia*, and broken up in Italy the following year.

Anchises (2) 1888 2,718 325.0x40.0x25.9 Triple Expansion 1,841 10 knots
B Wigham Richardson, Newcastle.
Originally Lund's Blue Anchor Line's *Wilcannia* and sold to Alfred Holt in 1897 and renamed *Anchises*. She was transferred to NSM 'Oceaan' the following year and returned to the British registry in 1906. Broken up at Briton Ferry in 1910.

Glaucus (2) 1896 5,570 423.1x49.0x38.3 Triple Expansion 3,583 10 knots
B Workman, Clark & Company, Belfast.
Prometheus class. She was torpedoed and sunk off Sicily on 3 June 1918.

Antenor (2) 1896 5,531 422.0x49.4x38.3 Triple Expansion 3,563 10 knots
B Workman, Clark & Company, Belfast.
Prometheus class. Transferred to NSM 'Oceaan' in 1914 but later returned to British flag. Torpedoed in the Mediterranean on 9 February 1918 but survived the attack. She was sold to INSA of Genoa in 1925, renamed *Fortunato*, and was broken up in Italy the following year.

Patroclus (2)/ Palamed (2) 1896 5,509 422.0x49.4x28.6 Triple Expansion 3,548 10 knots
B Workman, Clark & Company, Belfast.
Prometheus class. Transferred to NSM 'Oceaan' in 1914 and renamed *Palamed* in 1923. Sold the following year to Atlantide SA per Imprese Marittima of Genoa, renamed *Australia* and broken up at Genoa in 1929.

Left: *Antenor* (2).

Below left: *Patroclus* (2).

Below right: *Stentor* (2).

Idomeneus 1899 6,764 441.8x52.6x30.3 Triple Expansion 4,299 10 knots
B Scott & Company, Greenock.
First of a class of nine ships. She was torpedoed and beached off the west coast of Scotland on 15 September 1917 and was repaired and brought back into service. Transferred to NSM 'Oceaan' in 1922 and sold to Ditta L. Pittaluga Vapori of Genoa in 1925 becoming *Aurania*. She was broken up at Genoa in 1933.

Calchas 1899 6,748 441.8x52.6x30.3 Triple Expansion 4,279 10 knots
B Scott & Company, Greenock.
Idomeneus class. She was torpedoed and sunk off Tearaght Island, Ireland, on 11 May 1917. All crew were saved.

Machaon 1899 6,738 441.8x52.6x30.3 Triple Expansion 4,277 10 knots
B Scott & Company, Greenock.
Idomeneus class. She was torpedoed and sunk off Cani Rocks, Tunisia, on 27 February 1918.

Stentor (2) 1899 6,773 441.8x52.6x30.3 Triple Expansion 4,308 10 knots
B Workman, Clark & Company, Belfast.
Idomeneus class. She was transferred to NSM 'Oceaan' in 1922 and sold to Madrigal & Company of Manila, Philippines, becoming *Don Jose*. She was broken up at Singapore three years later.

Alcinous 1900 6692 441.8x52.6x30.3 Triple Expansion 4,250 10 knots
B Scott & Company, Greenock.
Idomeneus class. She was requisitioned by the Admiralty at the beginning of the First World War and was used as a Squadron Supply Ship. On 31 March 1918, she was hit by a torpedo fired from UB-57 on a voyage from London

Right: Agamemnon (2).

Far right: Peleus.

to Boston. Towed to a Thames anchorage and later to Tilbury, where she was repaired. She also saw action on 2 September that year, when she was again attacked by a submarine in the western Atlantic. Her crew returned the fire and the submarine turned around and left the scene. In 1925, she was sold to Ditta L. Pittaluga Vapori of Genoa and renamed *Carmania*. Her name was changed to *Silvania* in 1928 and she was broken up at Genoa in 1932.

Agamemnon (2) 1900 7,010 442.1x52.7x32.0 Triple Expansion 4,461 10 knots
B Scott & Company, Greenock.
Idomeneus class. She was attacked by U-48 on 16 July 1917, but her superior speed enabled her to escape the German submarine. Sold to Soc. Anon. Commerciale Italo-Chilena in 1927, renamed *Impero* and broken up at Genoa in 1932.

Ajax (2) 1900 7,043 442.5x52.7x32.0 Triple Expansion 4,484 10 knots
B Scott & Company, Greenock.
Idomeneus class. *Ajax* was two years old when she grounded on the Jeddah Reef and filled with water but was salvaged and returned to service. She was requisitioned by the Admiralty in the First World War as an Expeditionary Force Transport and was attacked by U-39 on 10 October 1915, west of Crete, and was rescued by a British destroyer. Between December 1918 and April 1919, she was employed carrying prisoners of war from Hull to Copenhagen and Belgian refugees to Antwerp. She was briefly used as a troopship in 1920 prior to returning to Alfred Holt and was broken up in Japan in 1930.

Achilles (2) 1900 7,043 442.0x52.7x32.0 Triple Expansion 4,484 10 knots
B Scott & Company, Greenock.
Idomeneus class. In April 1915, she was requisitioned by the Admiralty and carried Indian troops between Alexandria and the Dardanelles, where she came under attack from Turkish batteries and two people were killed. She was also used as a reception ship for wounded servicemen and rescued forty-nine survivors from the troopship *Royal Edward*, which sank in the Aegean Sea with a loss of 132 crew and over 700 soldiers on 13 August 1915. On a voyage from Sydney to London and Liverpool on 31 March 1916, she was torpedoed and sunk by U-44 off Ushant and five lives were lost.

Deucalion (2) 1900 7,010 442.1x52.7x32.0 Triple Expansion 4,461 10 knots
B Scott & Company, Greenock.
Idomeneus class. After thirty years of service to the Blue Funnel Line, she was sold to Ditta L. Pittaluga Vapori of Genoa and sailed from Liverpool on 31 January 1930 under the name of *Aquitania*. She was broken up at Genoa three years later.

Atlanta 1899 107 86.0x17.1x8.6 Compound 37 —
She was used for harbour duties and tendering services at Hong Kong, bought by the Ocean Steamship Company in 1902, and was sold to Tang Luk of Hong Kong in 1923 and renamed *Moon Tong*. Sold to Chinese interests in 1927, and used as a barge at Hong Kong.

Peleus 1901 7,441 454.7x54.1x32.3 Triple Expansion 4,800 10 knots
B Workman, Clark & Company, Belfast.
First of a class of four ships. She was launched on 23 February 1901 but failed to enter the water until a week later, when her launch was completed. At Greenock on 21 September 1915, she was in collision with the *Marchioness* and the tug *Flying Wizard*. In April 1931, she was sold to Madrigal & Company of Manila, renamed *Perseus* and was broken up at Osaka in Japan two years later.

Jason (2) in dazzle paint during the First World War. Exact date and location unknown.

Tydeus 1901 7,441 454.7x54.1x32.3 Triple Expansion 4,800 10 knots
B Workman, Clark & Company, Belfast.
Peleus class. She gave thirty years of uneventful service to the company and was broken up by Smith & Houston at Port Glasgow in 1931.

Telemachus (2) 1902 7,450 454.7x54.1x32.3 Triple Expansion 4,802 10 knots
B Workman, Clark & Company, Belfast.
Peleus class. On 7 May 1910, she was 464 miles west of Minikoi Island and the crew caught sight of a small boat, which contained one man who was alive and another dead man. The survivor was Joshua Green, who told them that he and two others had set out to cross from one Seychelles island to another but had become lost. He told them that another steamer had stopped and gave them the correct course but they soon realised that they were lost again. Green was 900 miles from his home and had been adrift in the boat for four months. *Telemachus* was sold to Ditta Luigi Pittaluga Vapori of Genoa in 1932, renamed *Tasmania* and was broken up in Italy the following year.

Jason (2) 1902 7,450 454.7x54.1x32.3 Triple Expansion 4,802 10 knots
B Workman, Clark & Company, Belfast.
Peleus class. *Jason* was requisitioned by the Admiralty in July 1915 and returned to the Ocean Steamship Company in March 1918. She was broken up in Japan in 1931.

Oopack 1894 3,883 370.0x45.3x27.0 Triple Expansion 2,517 10 knots
B Workman, Clark & Company, Belfast, for the China Mutual Steam Navigation Company, Liverpool.
The fleet was taken over by Alfred Holt in 1902. On 4 October 1918, east of Malta, the ship was hit in No. 1 and No. 2 holds by torpedoes. The ship had left Milo, Greece, on 2 October under the command of Captain D. T. Williams in a seven-ship convoy heading to Malta. The ships were escorted by HMS *Snapdragon* and a submarine was seen following the convoy. It was UB-68, which was commanded by Lt.-Cdr Karl Dönitz, and following the attack, *Snapdragon* followed the submarine, which surfaced close to her. The first shell fired from *Snapdragon* demolished the conning tower and UB-68 surrendered. The survivors from *Oopack* and UB-68 were transferred to *Snapdragon* and Dönitz believed that he had sunk two ships. As *Snapdragon* entered Valletta, the survivors lined the deck and Dönitz ordered his men to remove their caps and they shouted 'Hoch der Kaiser' ('up the Kaiser'). *Oopack* was the last Blue Funnel vessel to be lost in the First World War.

Ching Wo 1894 3,883 370.0x45.3x27.0 Triple Expansion 2,517 10 knots
B Workman, Clark & Company, for the China Mutual Steam Navigation Company, Liverpool.
The fleet was taken over by Alfred Holt in 1902 and *Ching Wo* was sold to Uchida Kisen KK, Tarumi, Japan, in 1911, becoming *Unkai Maru* No. 2. She was sold to the French Government in 1920, renamed *Indochine* and broken up in 1923.

Kaisow 1895 3,921 370.0x46.0x28.3 Triple Expansion 2,529 10 knots
B D. & W. Henderson, Glasgow, for the China Mutual Steam Navigation Company, Liverpool.
Taken over by Alfred Holt in 1902 and sold to Kanamori Gomei Kaisha, Amagasaki, Japan, in 1911 and renamed *Shintsu Maru*. She was renamed *Toyo Maru* in 1919 and purchased by A/D Gylfe in 1921, renamed *Alssund*, and managed by T. C. Christensen of Copenhagen. She was broken up in 1923.

Pak Ling (2) 1895 4,614 410.0x48.1x27.4 Triple Expansion 2,875 10 knots
B Workman, Clark & Company, Belfast, for the China Mutual Steam Navigation Company, Liverpool.
Taken over by Alfred Holt in 1902. On 6 July 1920, she went ashore in fog off Button Island, Bonham Straits, south of Shanghai, and was refloated on 13 July with the aid of the Shanghai Tug & Lighterage Company tug *St Dominic*. Repairs were carried out at Shanghai, and she traded for another three years before she was broken up at Wilhemshaven in 1923.

Kintuck 1895 4,447 410.0x48.1x27.4 Triple Expansion 2,881 10 knots
B Workman, Clark & Company, Belfast, for the China Mutual Steam Navigation Company, Liverpool.
Taken over by Alfred Holt in 1902. On 2 December 1916, she was attacked by a German submarine off south-west Ireland but managed to escape and was also attacked on 13 June 1917 and escaped again. However, she was again torpedoed on 2 December that year and sank off Godrevy Lighthouse, Cornwall.

Moyune 1895 4,646 410.0x48.1x26.2 Triple Expansion 3,016 10 knots
B D. & W. Henderson, Glasgow, for the China Mutual Steam Navigation Company, Liverpool.
Taken over by Blue Funnel Line in 1902. She was blown ashore on 14 April 1897 at Castle Haven, near St Catherines in the Isle of Wight following an engine failure. She was refloated and returned to service. In 1915, she was requisitioned by the British Government and carried goods and cargo to Canada, Burma, Egypt and the United States. On 12 April 1918, she was torpedoed and sunk by U-34 near Cape Palos, Cartagena, Spain, on a voyage from Karachi to Liverpool.

Teenkai 1895 4,642 410.0x48.1x26.2 Triple Expansion 3,016 10 knots
B D. & W. Henderson, Glasgow.
Built for the China Mutual Steam Navigation Company, Liverpool. Taken over by Alfred Holt in 1902 and sold to 'Globus' Rheederei AG, Bremen, in 1922, and renamed *Gerfrid*. Bought by Pereira Carneiro & Cia, Rio de Janeiro, Brazil, in 1927, becoming *Merity*.

Yangtsze 1899 6,457 450.0x53.2x30.9 Triple Expansion 4,149 10 knots
B Workman, Clark & Company, Belfast, for the China Mutual Steam Navigation Company, Liverpool.
Taken over by Alfred Holt in 1902. On 25 April 1918, she survived a torpedo attack, west of Gibraltar, and was sold to Madrigal & Company of Manila in 1927, renamed *Macaria* and was broken up in Japan in 1933.

Teenkai.

Ping Suey.

Ping Suey 1899 6,458 450.0x53.2x30.9 Triple Expansion 4,150 10 knots
B Workman, Clark & Company, Belfast, for the China Mutual Steam Navigation Company, Liverpool.
Taken over by Alfred Holt in 1902. On 24 June 1916, on a voyage from Liverpool to Durban, she went aground on Dassen Island, Cape of Good Hope, and the crew ate penguin eggs while they were waiting to be rescued. As the company carried their own insurance, the rules laid down concerning navigation practice were precise and strict. However, it has been reported that, on this voyage, the longitude established by the second mate was one degree west of the true position. The ship was 50 miles closer to Dassen Island than had been calculated. The design of the wheelhouse was different to most company vessels, and consequently, there was no view forward from the chartroom. To further complicate issues, the bosun had organised painting work near the bridge and tarpaulin was obscuring the view ahead by the helmsman. At 15.00, the ship grounded and lay there until 1917, when she was salvaged and then sold to

Far left: Hyson.

Left: Oanfa (2).

Lloyd de Pacifico, Savona, and renamed *Attalita*. She survived a torpedo attack west of Gibraltar on 25 April 1918 and was broken up at Genoa in 1932.

Hyson 1899 6,608 450.0x53.2x30.9 Triple Expansion 4,232 10 knots
B Workman, Clark & Company, Belfast, for the China Mutual Steam Navigation Company, Liverpool.
Taken over by Alfred Holt in 1902. On 29 May 1917, she was followed by a German U-boat in the English Channel but escaped undamaged. In 1926, she was sold to E. Bozzo and L. Mortola of Genoa, renamed *Maria Rosa*, and broken up at Spezia in 1932.

Keemun 1902 9,067 482.0x58.2x32.8 Triple Expansion 5,727 10 knots
B Workman, Clark & Company, Belfast, for the China Mutual Steam Navigation Company, Liverpool. She was taken over while on the stocks. On 13 June 1918, she was attacked by a German submarine and survived by the accurate gunnery of her crew. During the war, she carried fuel oil in her ballast tanks from the Far East to Britain. She survived until 1933, when she was broken up in Japan.

Ningchow 1902 8,813 482.0x58.2x32.8 Triple Expansion 5,716 10 knots
B D. & W. Henderson, Glasgow, for the China Mutual Steam Navigation Company, Liverpool.
She had a long, uneventful life and was broken up at Spezia, Italy, where she arrived on 4 November 1932.

Oanfa (2) 1903 7,602 482.0x58.2x32.8 Triple Expansion 4,867 10 knots
B D. & W. Henderson, Glasgow, for the China Mutual Steam Navigation Company, Liverpool. She gave nearly thirty years service to the company and was broken up in 1932.

Oanfa (1)/Rhipeus 1888 3,061 325.5x47.2x22.5 Triple Expansion 1,950 10 knots
B Aitken & Mansel, Glasgow. She was built for the China Shippers Company and became part of the China Mutual Steam Navigation Company in 1893. In 1900, she was bought by NSM 'Oceaan' and renamed *Rhipeus*. Sold to NG Pittaluga of Genoa in 1910, renamed *Ginolia* and broken up in Genoa in 1911.

Memnon (2) 1888 2,458 320.0x40.3x22.6 Triple Expansion 1,560 10 knots
B Hawthorn, Leslie & Company, Newcastle.
Built as *Gulf of Guinea* for Gulf Line, Greenock (later renamed the Greenock Steamship Company). She was bought by Alfred Holt in 1899 and took the name *Memnon*. Transferred to NSM 'Oceaan' in 1900 and sold to K. Watanabe, Hakodate, and renamed *Togo Maru* No. 1 and later *Togo Maru*. On a voyage from Tsingtao to Yokohama with a cargo of coal, coke and cattle, she was wrecked off Mokpo in Korea on 20 July 1923.

Charon 1903 2,682 306.1x45.2x19.6 Triple Expansion 1,661 12 knots
B Caledon Shipbuilding Company, Dundee.
Built for the Singapore to Batavia and Fremantle joint service with the West Australian Steam Navigation Company and flew both companies house flags. Sold to Yuang Heng Steamship Company of China in 1925 and was renamed *Yuan Lee*. In 1935, she was renamed *King Lee*, and when sold to Kwang Tung Product Sales Bureau of Canton, she became *Wing Fook*. Purchased by

Priam (3).

Telamon (2).

Bellerophon (2).

Wallem & Company of Hong Kong in 1941, becoming *Iris* of Panamanian registry. Following the end of the Second World War, she was purchased by Chinese interests and renamed *Hsiang Hsing*. She was beached at Keelung on 7 March 1950, when she began to sink. Refloated and towed to dry dock, where temporary repairs were made, she later sank again in Keelung Harbour on 12 August that year.

Gorgon 1908 2,885 300.0x42.0x26.6 Triple Expansion 1,734 12 knots
B Scott's Shipbuilding & Engineering Company, Greenock.
Built to operate with *Charon* (1). Requisitioned by the Admiralty in 1917 and operated in the Mediterranean as an Expeditionary Force Transport. Purchased by Cheong Hing Steamship Company of Hong Kong in 1928 and renamed *Lyeemoon* and used as an emigrant ship in Chinese and South-East Asian waters. She is reported as being wrecked at Benghazi on 4 January 1943.

Priam (3) 1904 4,543 382.7x47.2x28.2 Triple Expansion 2,905 10 knots
B Hawthorn, Leslie & Company, Newcastle.
Broken up in Japan in 1931.

Laertes (2) 1904 4,541 382.7x47.2x28.2 Triple Expansion 2,904 10 knots
B Hawthorn, Leslie & Company, Newcastle.
Priam class. Survived an attack by a German U-boat off the Dutch coast on 10 February 1915. However, she was torpedoed and sunk off Prawl Point on 1 August 1917 when fourteen of her crew were lost.

Telamon (2) 1904 4,509 382.7x47.2x28.2 Triple Expansion 2,843 10 knots
B Workman, Clark & Company, Belfast.
Priam class. After twenty-nine years of service, she was sold to Douglas & Ramsey in 1933 and then broken up by Smith & Houston at Port Glasgow.

Bellerophon (2) 1906 8,954 485.3x58.3x31.0 Triple Expansion 5,744 10 knots
B Workman, Clark & Company, Belfast.
The first of a class of six vessels known as 'goal post' ships. They entered service on the newly acquired China Mutual route from Glasgow and Liverpool to Singapore, China, Japan, Vancouver and Seattle. *Bellerophon* was the only vessel of the class to have steel decks, as the others were built with wooden decks. In 1914, she was taken over by the Admiralty as a British Expeditionary Force troopship and horse carrier, operating from Liverpool to France.

She became a troop carrier again in 1927 when she loaded troops, 750 horses and supplies in February at Birkenhead for Hong Kong and Shanghai. She sailed with P&O's *Karmala* and Aberdeen Line's *Herminius*, stopping at Port Said to refuel. Her career ended when she arrived at Barrow on 18 April 1948 to be broken up by Thos. W. Ward.

Teucer (3) 1906 9,017 485.3x58.3x31.0 Triple Expansion 5,805 14 knots
B Hawthorn, Leslie & Company, Newcastle.
Bellerophon class. Although they were known as the *Bellerophon*-class, *Teucer* was the first to enter service and was the fastest ship. She avoided an attack by a U-boat in the Mediterranean in December 1915 and arrived at Troon on 10 January 1948 to be broken up by W. H. Arnott Young & Company.

Far left: Teucer (3).

Left: Antilochus.

Far left: Cyclops (2).

Left: Titan (2).

Antilochus 1906 9,011 485.3x58.3x31.0 Triple Expansion 5,796 14 knots
B Hawthorn, Leslie & Company, Newcastle.
Bellerophon class. Survived an attack by a U-boat in the Mediterranean on 10 September 1915. She came to the rescue of the survivors of Mentor when she sank off Florida on 29 May 1942, arrived at Briton Ferry on 11 April 1948 to be broken up.

Cyclops (2) 1906 8,998 485.3x58.3x31.0 Triple Expansion 5,748 14 knots
B D. & W. Henderson & Company, Glasgow.
Bellerophon class. On 11 February 1917, she was in view of a German submarine off southern Ireland but managed to escape, and on 11 April, she narrowly escaped an attack by another submarine after a torpedo was fired at her west of the Scilly Islands. When she was 200 miles off Cape Sable on the 11 January 1942 she was torpedoed by U-123 and sank. Forty six passengers and 41crew were lost.

Titan (2) 1906 8,954 485.3x58.3x31.0 Triple Expansion 5,720 14 knots
B D. & W. Henderson & Company, Glasgow.
Bellerophon class. On a light voyage from London to Sydney on 3/4 September 1940, she was torpedoed at midnight by U-47 north-west of Rockall. Six of her crew were lost but ninety were rescued by HMS *Godetia* and HMCS *St Laurent*.

Protesilaus 1910 9,547 484.9x60.4x39.5 Triple Expansion 6,116 14 knots
B Hawthorn, Leslie & Company, Newcastle.
Bellerophon class. She was mined in the Bristol Channel off Swansea on 21 January 1940 and towed into port, where she was found to be beyond economic repair. Broken up by Thos. W. Ward at Briton Ferry in 1942.

Myrmidon (2) 1905 4,965 391.5x49.2x28.8 Triple Expansion 3063 10 knots
B Armstrong, Whitworth & Company, Newcastle, completed for the China Mutual Steam Navigation Company, Liverpool.

Protesilaus.

Myrmidon (2).

Theseus.

She was requisitioned by the Admiralty in 1915 as an Expeditionary Force Transport and a naval collier. She was damaged by a torpedo fired by U-69 in the Irish Sea on 24 July 1917 but managed to limp back to Liverpool.

On 7 September that year, she was beached at Phillippeville following a torpedo attack by U-54 and was later refloated and arrived at Algiers on 4 January 1918 to be repaired. She later returned to service and was sold to Marittiama Ravenate SA,Ravenna, in 1930 and renamed *Rubicone*. She survived until 1959, when she was broken up at Split.

Astyanax 1906 4,872 391.5x49.2x28.8 Triple Expansion 3,021 10 knots
B Scott & Company, Greenock.
Myrmidon class. On 9 December 1916, she was followed by a German submarine off southern Ireland but managed to escape and also escaped an attack by a submarine off south-west Ireland on 9 May the following year. She was sold to Oscar Limited, converted to a coal hulk for work in Singapore Harbour in 1930 and renamed *Oscar* II. As the Japanese attacked Hong Kong, she was scuttled in the harbour on 18 February 1942 and the wreckage was removed after the war.

Memnon (3) 1906 4,870 391.5x49.2x28.8 Triple Expansion 3,019 10 knots
B Scott & Company, Greenock.
Myrmidon class. Completed for the China Mutual Steam Navigation Company, Liverpool. She was used as an Expeditionary Force Transport in the Mediterranean at times during the First World War. She served the company until 1930, when she was broken up at Kobe.

Polyphemus (2) 1906 4,807 391.5x49.2x28.8 Triple Expansion 3,019 10 knots
B Armstrong, Whitworth & Company, Newcastle.
Myrmidon class. Completed for the China Mutual Steam Navigation Company, Liverpool. She escaped a torpedo attack by U-66, off the south-west of Scotland on 20 July 1917 and another the following day by U-58 off the coast of Ireland. In 1923, she was converted to diesel power and was broken up at Kobe in 1930.

Perseus 1908 6,728 443.0x52.9x32.0 Triple Expansion 4,299 11 knots
B Workman, Clark & Company, Belfast.
The first of a class of nine vessels. On 29 March 1915, she escaped from a torpedo attack off the Scilly Islands and was sunk by a mine which had been laid by the German raider *Wolf* off Colombo on 21 February 1917.

Theseus 1908 6,723 443.0x52.9x32.0 Triple Expansion 4,297 11 knots
B Workman, Clark & Company, Belfast.
Perseus class. On 29 March 1915, she was fired on by U-28 off the Scilly Islands but escaped after returning the gunfire. Sold to Thos. W. Ward to be broken up at Preston in 1947 and ran aground in the River Ribble. Two months later, she was refloated and towed to the breakers' yard on 30 November.

Neleus 1911 6,685 443.0x52.9x32.0 Triple Expansion 4,260 11 knots
B Workman, Clark & Company, Belfast, for the China Mutual Steam Navigation Company, Liverpool.
Perseus class. Sold to the British Iron & Steel Corportion and broken up by Thos. W. Ward at Preston, where she arrived on 1 November 1948.

Demodocus.

Laomedon.

Atreus 1911 6,728 443.0x52.9x32.0 Triple Expansion 4,299 11 knots
B Scott's Shipbuilding & Engineering Company, Greenock, for the China Mutual Steam Navigation Company, Liverpool.
Perseus class. Sold to the British Iron & Steel Corporation and arrived at Rosyth on 3 October 1949 to be broken up.

Rhesus 1911 6719 443.0x52.9x32.0 Triple Expansion 4,280 11 knots
B Scott's Shipbuilding & Engineering Company, Greenock, for the China Mutual Steam Navigation Company, Liverpool.
Perseus class. On 14 July 1917, she was attacked off the south-west of Ireland, but the torpedo missed her. She survived both world wars and was finally broken up in 1950.

Demodocus 1912 6,689 443.0x52.9x32.0 Triple Expansion 4,269 11 knots
B Workman, Clark & Company, Belfast, for the China Mutual Steam Navigation Company, Liverpool.
Perseus class. She was taken over by the Liner Requisition Scheme in 1917 and was torpedoed in the Mediterranean on 23 March 1918, when five people were lost. She was towed to Malta for repairs and survived the rest of the war without any major incident. In 1932, she was transferred to the Australian service, and in January 1949, she towed *Lycaon* (1), which had lost her propeller, 850 miles from Cape Town. It was later calculated that *Demodocus* lost twenty days voyage time and a claim was made against *Lycaon* for the loss of £128 per day and an extra 1,154 tons of coal and general salvage. The Court of Admiralty awarded £12,500 to the company, £350 to the captain and £2,400 to be divided among the crew.

She was sold two years later to Ditta Luigi Pittaluga Vapori, renamed *Ircania* and sold again to P. Tomei of Genoa in 1956, becoming *Miriam*. On 10 October 1958, she arrived at Trieste to be broken up.

Laomedon 1912 6,693 443.0x52.9x32.0 Triple Expansion 4,268 11 knots
B Workman, Clark & Company, Belfast, for the China Mutual Steam Navigation Company, Liverpool.
Perseus class. In the First World War, she carried cargoes for India, Portugal, France, Serbia and Russia and carried out trooping duties in the Mediterranean. On 2 April 1916, she fought off an attack by a German U-boat in the Mediterranean and survived the Second World War unscathed. On 22 December 1949, she arrived at Faslane to be broken up by Shipbreaking Industries Limited.

Eumaeus 1913 6,696 443.0x52.9x32.0 Triple Expansion 4,266 11 knots
B Workman, Clark & Company, Belfast.
Perseus class. On 6 February 1917 at 19.00, *Tyndareus* was mined off Cape Agulhas by mines that had been laid by *Wolf*. The 25th Middlesex Rifle Regiment, who were on board *Tyndareus*, were transferred to the hospital ship *Oxfordshire* and the *Eumaeus*, which were standing by the stricken vessel. *Tyndareus* was later towed into Cape Town. On 26 February the following year, she was torpedoed and sank near Ile de Vierge.

Helenus.

Teiresias.

Phemius 1913 6,699 443.0x52.9x32.0 Triple Expansion 4,268 11 knots
B Workman, Clark & Company, Belfast.
Perseus class. She was the last of the class. On 4 June 1917, she was torpedoed and sank off Eagle Island, Ireland.

Lycaon 1913 7,552 455.3x56.3x32.5 Triple Expansion 4,814 11 knots
B Hawthorn, Leslie & Company, Newcastle for the China Mutual Steam Navigation Company, Liverpool.
In January 1949, she lost her propeller in the Indian Ocean and was towed to Cape Town by *Demodocus* (1). She was transferred to the Glen Line two years later, becoming *Gleniffer*, and arrived at Faslane to be broken up on 7 July 1952.

Helenus 1913 7,555 455.3x56.3x32.5 Triple Expansion 4,810 11 knots
B Scott's Shipbuilding & Engineering Company, Greenock.
Lycaon class. Requisitioned by the Admiralty in 1917-18 as an Expeditionary Force Transport and carried Portuguese troops. She was torpedoed by the German U-boat U-53 in the English Channel on 1 December 1917 and was towed into port. On 30 June the following year, she escaped a torpedo fired at her in the North Sea, and on 22 August, she was followed and fired on by U-90, but her speed helped her to escape. She was torpedoed and sunk by U-68 off Freetown on 3 March 1942; five of her crew were lost.

Troilus 1913 7,562 455.3x56.3x32.5 Triple Expansion 4,814 11 knots
Lycaon class. In her first year of service, on a voyage from Yokohama to London, she was sunk by the German cruiser *Emden* on 19 October 1914 off Minikoi Island in the Indian Ocean. This was Alfred Holt's first war loss.

Teiresias 1914 7,606 455.3x56.3x32.5 Triple Expansion 4,822 11 knots
B Hawthorn, Leslie & Company, Newcastle.
Lycaon class. On 30 June 1915, she was damaged when she collided with a mine in the Suez Canal. She was on a voyage from Avonmouth to Quiberon Bay on 17 June 1940, when she was bombed by German aircraft off St Nazaire. The first bomb flooded the engine-room and stokehold, causing a crack across the main deck and down the port side of the vessel. The crew were ordered to standby the lifeboats and by the next day she had a 25-degree list and rivets were heard to be popping out of the hull. When she was again attacked from the air, she capsized and sank. The crew in the boats made their way to St Nazaire and were brought back to Britain by HMS *Oracle* and those who remained on board were taken off by *Holmside*.

Agapenor 1914 7,587 455.3x56.3x32.5 Triple Extension 4,798 11 knots
B Scott's Shipbuilding & Engineering Company, Greenock.
Lycaon class. On a voyage from Karachi to Britain on 10 October 1942, she rescued the survivors from the *Glendene*. However, she was torpedoed the following day by U-87 south-west of Freetown. Her captain, P. W. Savery, had

Above left: Agapenor.

Above right: Pyrrhus (2).

Left: Diomed (3).

survived the sinking of the *Helenus* earlier that year. He was picked up by another vessel but seven of her crew were lost.

Mentor 1914 7,585 455.3x56.3x32.5 Triple Expansion 4,798 11 knots
B Scott's Shipbuilding & Engineering Company, Greenock.
Lycaon class. On 28 May 1942, she was torpedoed by U-106 off Key West, Florida. She was carrying war materials from New Orleans to Bombay via Cape Town. The torpedo struck the engine-room on the port side, causing flooding. Seven of her crew were killed and a second torpedo exploded causing severe damage. The survivors were picked up by *Antilochus* (1).

Pyrrhus (2) 1914 7,615 455.3x56.3x32.5 Triple Expansion 4,823 11 knots
B Workman, Clark & Company, Belfast.
Lycaon class. She was torpedoed off Cape Finisterre by U-37 on a voyage from the Clyde and Liverpool to Gibraltar and Manila on 17 February 1940 as part of a Convoy. The ship broke in two, with the fore part floating for about two days and the aft section sinking quickly. Eight of her crew of eighty-five were lost and the survivors were picked up by the *Ukside* and *Sinnington Court*.

Troilus (2) 1917 7,625 455.3x56.3x32.5 Triple Expansion 4,832 11 knots
B Caledon Shipbuilding & Engineering Company, Dundee.
Lycaon class. She was followed by a German submarine in the North Sea on 11 April 1917 and was torpedoed and sunk 140 miles off Malin Head on 2 May that year.

Diomed (3) 1917 7,523 455.0x56.3x32.5 Triple Expansion 4,747 11 knots
B Scott's Shipbuilding & Engineering Company, Greenock.
Lycaon class. Attacked and sunk by U-140 off Nantucket lightship on 21 August 1918.

Elpenor 1917 7,601 455.3x56.3x32.5 Triple Expansion 4,824 11 knots
B Hawthorn, Leslie & Company, Newcastle, for the China Mutual Steam Navigation, Liverpool.
Lycaon class. She sailed on her maiden voyage from Newcastle to the Mediterranean and Baltimore after she had been placed under the Liner Requisition Scheme. In November 1918, she carried troops between Liverpool and Dublin and was returned to her owners on the completion of hostilities. In 1922, she collided with the Japanese vessel *Inaba Maru* at Kobe and was transferred to the Glen Line in 1935, becoming *Glenfinlas*. She was damaged by an air attack off Harwich in November 1941, and the following November, damaged by bombs in Bougie Harbour while taking part in the North African landings, named Operation *Torch*. She was set on fire and sunk and was raised in 1943 and was later towed to Oran for temporary repairs to be completed. It was decided to bring her back to Sunderland via Gibraltar for permanent repairs, and she was returned to the Blue Funnel Line in April 1947 as *Elpenor*. Transferred again to the Glen Line in 1950, becoming *Glenfinlas*, she was broken up at Blyth by Hughes Bolckow in 1952.

Autolycus 1917 5,806 423.8x52.3x29.9 Triple Expansion 3,664 10 knots
B Taikoo Dockyard & Engineering Company, Hong Kong.
She was on her first voyage from Hong Kong to Liverpool when she was torpedoed and sunk by U-34 off Cape Palos, Sardinia, on 12 April 1918.

Laertes (3) 1919 5,868 423.8x52.3x29.9 Triple Expansion 3,647 10 knots
B Taikoo Dockyard & Engineering Company, Hong Kong.
Transferred to NSM 'Oceaan' in 1922. On 3 May 1942, she was torpedoed by U-564 off Cape Canaveral on a voyage from New York to Bombay via Cape Town. Eighteen of the crew were lost.

Aeneas 1910 10,049 493.0x60.0x29.0 Triple Expansion 6,300 14 knots
B Workman, Clark & Company, Belfast.
She sailed on her maiden voyage on 18 November 1910 from Glasgow, Liverpool and Fishguard to Las Palmas, Cape Town, Adelaide, Melbourne, Sydney and Brisbane. The Australian service operated on a six-week basis, took thirty-nine days and the ships called at Fremantle and Durban on the homeward voyage. In 1914, she operated for the Australian Government as a troopship and ran aground in May 1918 at Torcor Head on Rathlin Island. She returned to the Australian service on 29 May 1920 with accommodation for 180 first class passengers, and in 1924, the service was operated jointly with White Star Line. The following year, *Aeneas* was transferred to the Far East service, joining the new *Sarpedon*, *Patroclus*, *Hector* and *Antenor*. On 2 July 1940, she was sunk by an air attack off Start Point, Plymouth, as she was heading from London to Glasgow to finish unloading her cargo. She was part of a convoy and was the largest ship in line. The main steam supply was severed and blew out her starboard side, and when fires broke out, Captain D. L. C. Evans ordered all crew to the boats just before she sank. Nineteen of her crew were lost, and the survivors were rescued by HMS *Worthington*.

Ascanius (2) 1910 10,048 493.0x60.0x29.0 Triple Expansion 6,777 14 knots
B Workman, Clark & Company, Belfast.
Aeneas class. She was placed on the Australian service and sailed on her maiden voyage on 30 December 1910 from Glasgow and Liverpool to

Above: Aeneas.

Right: Ascanius (2).

Brisbane. She operated as an Expeditionary Force Transport in 1914 as a troopship for the Australian Government and was taken over by the Liner Requisition Scheme in 1917. *Ascanius* returned to the Australian service for her owners on 21 August 1920 and was sent to Palmer's at Jarrow two years later for a major refit. In 1940, she was requisitioned again as a troopship, and on 30 July 1944, she was torpedoed but managed to get back to Liverpool and was repaired by Cammell Laird. The following year, she was employed to carry Jewish emigrants from Marseilles to Haifa and was sold in 1949 to Cia. De Nav.'Florencia' of Genoa for a proposed service to carry emigrants to Australia, and was renamed *San Giovannino*. However, she was never used for this purpose and was laid up and broken up in 1952 at La Spezia.

Anchises (3) 1911 10,046 493.0x60.0x29.0 Triple Expansion 6,380 14 knots
B Workman, Clark & Company, Belfast.
Aeneas class. Requisitioned for trooping duties in 1914. On 23 September 1918, she was attacked by a German submarine and was able to return the fire, damaging the U-boat, which soon left the scene. She returned to her owner's Australian service in September 1922, sailing from Glasgow and Liverpool to Brisbane, and was damaged by an air attack off the east coast of Ireland on 27 February 1941 and lost power. The captain ordered that 134 passengers and crew abandon the ship, leaving a skeleton crew on board to attempt to take her to Liverpool. However, she was attacked again the following day when only 70 miles from the Mersey, sank, and twelve of her crew were killed. The other survivors were rescued by HMS *Kingcup* and HMCS *Assiniboine*.

Talthybius 1912 10,224 506.0x60.3x39.5 Triple Expansion 6,526 11 knots
B Scott's Shipbuilding & Engineering Company, Greenock.
The first ship of a class of four which were designed for the carriage of bulk cargoes able to be unloaded at ports unable to take deep-draft vessels. She was built with ten watertight bulkheads, subdividing the ship into nine cargo holds and associated 'tween decks. The hull was designed with a combination of framing, providing great transverse strength by substituting widely spaced, deep, heavy frames for the more conventional narrowly spaced frames, adding side stringers for longitudinal strength. She was fitted with twenty-seven derricks, of 2 tons, 10 tons and 15 tons, plus a 45-ton heavy-lift derrick and twenty-six steam winches. Accomodation for 600 steerage class passengers in the upper 'tween decks was also provided to attract pilgrims sailing to Jeddah. First class passenger accommodation was provided abaft of the master's cabin. On 4 and 8 May 1941, she received direct hits by bombs during air raids at Liverpool docks. She was berthed at Singapore on 3 February 1942 after arriving from Bombay, and with the close presence of the Japanese, the Chinese crew deserted. Discharge of her military cargo was undertaken by the officers and crew that remained, assisted by members of the Royal New Zealand Air Force, but she was bombed by Japanese aircraft. One New Zealand warrant officer was killed and six others, including one of the ship's gunners, were severely burned. The ship was assessed to be unseaworthy, as the pumps were unable to cope with the compartments steadily filling with water, and she sank. Further steady pumping lifted *Talthybius* off the bottom and the ship was towed to Empire Dock, where the pumps failed and she sank again. She

Anchises (3).

Talthybius.

was abandoned when Captain Kent ordered his men ashore to be rescued by HMS *Ping Wo*, which took them to Australia. *Ping Wo* arrived at Fremantle on 4 March, averaging about five knots over the seventeen days from Batavia. The master of *Talthybius* was awarded the OBE and the third officer was lost in 1944, when the *Empire Lancer* was torpedoed by a Japanese submarine off Madagascar. The radio officer survived the Japanese prison he was sent to and was brought back to the United Kingdom at the end of the war. *Talthybius* was later salvaged by the Japanese and renamed *Taruyasu Maru*. On 30 June 1945, she was mined off the north coast of Honshu. She was salvaged at the end of the war, repaired at Hong Kong in 1948 and renamed *Empire Evenlode*. In December that year, it was decided to bring her back to the United Kingdom with cargo from Singapore, and because her Suez Canal Certificate had long expired, she sailed around the Cape of Good Hope. As her call sign VRJT had not been updated in the line's other vessels' manuals, she was constantly being asked her name. When this was revealed to other ships of the line, they were showered with 'Welcome back' messages. The ship called at Mombasa, Durban and Cape Town, and a Union Castle liner passed them three times as the ship was only managing a few knots an hour. It took twenty-nine days to reach Swansea from Cape Town, arriving at Briton Ferry on 7 September 1949 to be broken up.

Ixion (2) 1912 10,229 506.0x60.3x39.5 Triple Expansion 6,527 11 knots
B Scott's Shipbuilding & Engineering Company for the China Mutual Steam Navigation Company, Liverpool.
Talthybius class. In 1918, she was employed carrying Serbian troops from Daini to Egypt and from Egypt to Basra. On a voyage from Glasgow to New York with a cargo of whisky, she was torpedoed by U-94 on 7 May 1941 in convoy, and sank the following day. The 105 survivors were rescued by the *Nailsea Manor* and an escort vessel.

Circe 1912 778 195.7x31.6x12.4 Triple Expansion 314 10 knots
B Taikoo Dockyard & Engineering Company, Hong Kong, for local feeder services at Singapore and transferred to the Straits Steamship Company in 1925.
She was taken over by the Admiralty in 1939, becoming HMS *Circe* and transferred to the Australian Navy in 1942 and renamed HMAS *Medea*. Sold and broken up at Sydney in 1946.

Medusa (2) 1913 793 195.7x31.6x12.4 Triple Expansion 323 10 knots
Sister of *Circe*. She was sold to the Straits Steamship Company in 1925 and was taken over by the Admiralty in 1939, becoming HMS *Medusa*. Transferred to the Australian Navy in 1942, renamed HMAS *Mercedes* and broken up at Sydney in 1945. The two sisters spent most of their lives together and were known affectionately as the 'heavenly twins', and when their service with the Australian Navy was over, they were tied up side by side.

Circe.

Nestor (3) 1913 14,500 563.2x68.4x31.2 Triple Expansion 9,100 13.5 knots
B Workman, Clark & Company, Belfast.
She cost £248,250 to build and sailed on her maiden voyage on 19 May 1913 from Glasgow and Liverpool to Cape Town, Adelaide, Melbourne, Sydney and Brisbane. She was taken over as a troopship in 1915, operating as an Australian Expedition Force Transport. Returned to her owners in 1920 for the Australian service, and steam superheaters were fitted the following year, improving engine economy. Her derrick vents were painted white in 1926, and her passenger capacity was reduced in 1935 from 250 to 175. In 1936, she was able to get a towing line to the *Mungana*, which was drifting towards rocks off Cape Jaffa, with her last rocket. She then towed the vessel 170 miles to Adelaide. Following the Second World War, her passenger accommodation was increased to 250 one class, carrying children being evacuated to Australia on her first voyage. On her last voyage, in 1949, she took five months, twenty days, compared to the four months it took on her maiden voyage. This was because of inferior coal and labour problems in Australia. She arrived at Faslane on 8 August 1950 to be broken up by Metal Industries Limited.

Above left: Nestor (3).

Above right: Ulysses (4).

Left: Eurymedon.

Ulysses (4) 1913 14,499 563.2x68.4x31.2 Triple Expansion 9,101 13.5 knots
B Workman, Clark & Company, Belfast for the China Mutual Steam Navigation Company, Liverpool.
Sister of *Nestor*. Employed on the Australian service, from Glasgow and Liverpool to Brisbane. She carried troops from Australia to Suez in 1915 and American soldiers across the North Atlantic in 1917. She was returned to Alfred Holt's Australian service in 1920 and was commanded by Captain R. D. Owen, OBE, in 1928, who was the commodore of the Blue Funnel Line. She was one of the last ships to leave Hong Kong before the Japanese invasion of the colony and sailed to Singapore and then to Australia to load for Liverpool. She sailed back across the Pacific, and after traversing the Panama Canal, she collided with a tanker in darkness on 8 April 1942 and was extensively damaged. She altered course for Newport News, and at 15.30 on 11 April, she was torpedoed by U-160 off Palm Beach, Florida. The torpedo struck hold No. 6 and the crew and passengers were ordered to abandon ship. A second torpedo hit her abreast of the funnel, and she quickly took in water and sank. There was no loss of life.

Eurydamas 1901 5,197 410.1x49.3x29.6 Triple Expansion 3,367 10 knots
B Chas. Connell & Company, Glasgow, for Thos. B. Royden & Company.
Built as *Indrasamha* and purchased by Blue Funnel Line in 1915 and named *Eurydamas*. This then gave them a place on the China to New York Conference. After nine years, she was sold to Jugoslavensko Amerikanska Plovidba of Split, renamed *Jugoslavija* in 1924, and was broken up at Genoa in 1934.

Eurymedon 1902 5,194 410.1x49.3x29.6 Triple Expansion 3,361 10 knots
B Chas. Connell & Company, Glasgow, for Thos. B. Royden & Company.
Eurydamas class. Built as *Indrawadi* and purchased in 1915 by Blue Funnel, becoming *Eurymedon*. In 1918, she was requisitioned by the Admiralty and was employed on a service to Canada and Karachi. She was sold to A/S Southern Queen, Thore Thoresen of Tonsberg, Norway, in 1922, renamed *Southern Queen* and was converted to a tanker. On 24 February 1928, she was lost in ice, east of South Orkney, took on water and sank. She was loading whale oil from whale catchers and 22,700 barrels were lost.

Eurybates.

Eurypylus.

Eurymachus 1906 4,995 400.6x52.3x29.3 Triple Expansion 3,214 10 knots
B Chas. Connell & Company, Glasgow, for Thos. B. Royden & Company.
Eurydamas class. Built as *Inverclyde* and acquired by Blue Funnel in 1915, becoming *Eurymachus*. She escaped an attack by a U-boat on 11 June 1917 and was sold to Jugoslavensko Amerikanska Plovidba of Rijeka, renamed *Nikola Mihanovic* and was broken up at Inverkeithing by Thos W. Ward in 1929.

Eurybates 1910 5529 430.2x50.2x30.7 Triple Expansion 3,507 10 knots
B Chas. Connell & Company, Glasgow, for Royden's Indra Line.
Built as *Indradeo* and purchased by the Blue Funnel Line in 1915, becoming *Eurybates*. She was sold in 1926 to R. & J. Thomas, Holyhead, renamed *Cambrian Peeress*, and transferred to William Thomas Shipping, managed by R. & J. Thomas in 1928. In 1931, she was bought by Ben Line, becoming *Benoran*, and was sunk at Arromanches as part of the Mulberry Harbour in June 1944. Three years later, she was salvaged and towed to Blyth, where she was broken up.

Eurypylus 1912 5,691 430.0x54.0x30.5 Triple Expansion 3,607 10 knots
B Chas. Connell & Company, Glasgow, for Royden's Indra Line.
Built as *Indrakuala*, bought by Ocean Steamship Company in 1915, and renamed *Eurypylus*. On 11 May 1918, she was in a collision and sank *Clan Mackay* west of the Scilly Islands. She was sold to the Continental Transit Company of London and renamed *Trade* in 1938 and was bought by the Board of Trade in 1939, becoming *Botavon*, and was later managed by the Ministry of Shipping, Ministry of War Transport. On a voyage from Middlesbrough to Reykjavik in convoy on 2 May 1942, she sank after being hit by an air-launched torpedo off North Cape in Norway.

Eurylochus 1912 5,723 430.5x53.9x30.3 Triple Expansion 3,600 10 knots
B London & Glasgow Shipbuilding Company, Glasgow, for Thos. B. Royden & Company.
Built as *Indraghira*, bought by Blue Funnel Line in 1915 and renamed *Eurylochus*. She was chased by a German U-boat on 22 July 1918 but escaped due to her speed. On a voyage from Liverpool to Takoradi on 29 January 1941, she received a message from the German Raider *Kormoran* (ex-*Steirmark*, Hamburg Amerika Line) telling her to heave to. *Eurylochus*'s Captain A. M. Caird ordered full steam ahead in an attempt to escape the German vessel, which fired star shells to illuminate the scene. The Blue Funnel vessel fired four shells, but receiving a direct hit, she came to a halt. The crew began to abandon the ship in the shark-infested waters, and the German vessel sent out a search party to examine *Eurylochus*'s cargo, which contained sixteen heavy bombers minus their engines. Captain Theodore Detmets decided to sink *Eurylochus* and fired a torpedo at her. When the torpedo was fired, it became clear that a lifeboat was alongside the British vessel with a number of crew who were attempting to get back on board. Detmets attempted to warn them that the torpedo had been fired, but as it exploded, the lifeboat and men disappeared. Thirty-eight of the crew were lost and the remaining forty-two were taken prisoner by *Kormoran*. HMS *Norfolk* and HMS *Devonshire* were dispatched

Euryades.

Tyndareus.

to the scene, but *Kormoran* had vanished when they arrived. The German Raider survived until 19 November 1941, when she was sunk by HMAS *Sydney*, which also sank.

Euryades 1913 5,713 430.0x54.0x30.5 Triple Expansion 3,620 10 knots
B Chas. Connell & Company, Glasgow, for Royden's Indra Line.
She was bought by the Ocean Steamship Company in 1915, becoming *Euryades*, and on 4 February 1918, she was fired on by a German U-boat, but the torpedo missed her. She was laid up for long periods between the wars and was sold to Thos. W. Ward for demolition at Briton Ferry in 1948.

Tyndareus 1916 11,347 507.0x63.2x41.0 Triple Expansion 7,172 12 knots
B Scott's Shipbuilding & Engineering Company, Greenock.
On 6 February 1917, she was mined off Cape Agulhas with the 25th Middlesex Rifle Regiment on board, who were ordered to row to the hospital ship *Oxfordshire* and the Blue Funnel vessel *Eumaeus*. *Tyndareus* was later towed stern first to Cape Town for emergency repairs to be carried out. In 1927, together with *Bellerophon*, she was used as a troop and horse carrier and was requisitioned as a troop and supply ship in the Second World War. In 1949, she was converted to a pilgrim ship at a cost of £126,650 and operated on the Indonesia to Mecca route the following year with accommodation for 2,500 pilgrims. When the pilgrim vessel *Gunang Djati* was introduced in 1960, *Tyndareus* was offered for sale and was broken up in Hong Kong later that year.

Knight of the Garter 1902 6,689 456.0x55.2x30.7 Triple Expansion 4,277 11 knots
B Chas. Connell & Company, Greenock, for the Knight Steamship Company, managed by Greenshields, Cowie & Company.
Chartered to Alfred Holt in 1914 and purchased in 1917. In the early years of the First World War, she operated in New Zealand as an Expeditionary Transport Force vessel, and under the French Government, she carried stores between Marseilles and Salonika, and carried wheat across the Atlantic for the British Government. On 11 February 1918, she was attacked by a German U-boat in the English Channel but escaped when the torpedoes failed to hit her. In 1923, she was sold to W. R. Davies & Company of Swansea and then to Emmanuel A. Stavroudis and became *Aspasia Stavroudi*. Three years later, she was purchased by NVSM 'Milligen' at Rotterdam, managed by G. A. Spliethoff and renamed *Hoffpiein*. She was wrecked on a voyage from Narvik to Rotterdam on 4 January 1930 off Skorpas Island, Norway.

Knight of the Thistle 1903 6,675 465.0x55.2x30.7 Triple Expansion 4,286 11 knots
B Chas. Connell & Company, Greenock; managed by Greenshields, Cowie & Co.
Knight of the Garter class. Purchased by Ocean Steamship Company in 1917 and attacked by a U-boat off south-west Ireland on 26 April that year. She foundered in the North Atlantic on 10 December 1917 on a voyage from New York to London.

Knight Templar.

Achilles (3).

Calchas (2)

Knight Templar 1905 7,175 470.0x58.0x31.8 Triple Expansion 4,602 11 knots
B Chas. Connell & Company, Glasgow; managed by Greenshields, Cowie & Co.
Bought by the Ocean Steamship Company in 1917 and torpedoed by U-53 south-west of the Eddystone Lighthouse on 7 April 1918 and later towed into Plymouth for repairs to be completed. Sold to A/S Tonsberg Hvalfangerei at Tonsberg in 1925, renamed *Orwell* and converted into a whale-oil carrier and floating refinery. She was broken up at Hamburg in 1954.

Knight Companion 1913 7,241 470.0x58.0x31.8 Triple Expansion 4,625 11 knots
B Chas. Connell & Company, Glasgow; managed by Greenshields, Cowie & Co.
Sister of *Knight Templar*. Requisitioned by the Admiralty as an Indian Expeditionary Force Transport, Royal Navy Collier No. 1389 and Expeditionary Force Transport No. F0186. On 10 January 1917, she returned fire with U-79 off Cape Finisterre and was purchased by the Ocean Steamship Company later that year. She was torpedoed in the Atlantic by the German submarine U-20 on 11 June that year and was towed back for repairs to be completed. At the end of the war, she was returned to the Ocean Steamship Company's service and was broken up in Italy in 1933.

Achilles (3) 1920 11,426 507.4x63.2x41.1 Triple Expansion 7,199 12 knots
B Scott's Shipbuilding & Engineering Company, Greenock.
Built for the Far East to United States service. She was used as a transport for horses and servicemen during the 'China Affair' in December 1926 and sailed to Shanghai. Sold to the Admiralty in 1940 and converted to a destroyer depot ship, she was renamed HMS *Blenheim*, armed with four 4-inch guns and a crew of 674 persons. Broken up at Barrow in 1948.

Philoctetes 1922 11,446 511.9x63.2x41.1 Triple Expansion 7,187 12 knots
B Scott's Shipbuilding & Engineering Company, Greenock, for the China Mutual Steam Navigation Company.
Sister of *Achilles*. Employed with *Achilles* on the Far East to United States service and was one of two Alfred Holt vessels at Yokohama in December 1923, when the city suffered a severe earthquake. The captain decided to leave the port and took the vessel to Kobe, a decision that was later criticised by the authorities. *Philoctetes* was also sold to the Admiralty in 1940 and converted to a destroyer depot ship as HMS *Philoctetes*. She was broken up at Newport, Monmouthshire, in 1948.

Calchas (2) 1921 10,304 490.8x62.4x39.6 Steam Turbine 6,313 14 knots
B Workman, Clark & Company, Belfast.
On a voyage from Sydney to Liverpool, she was torpedoed by U-107 on 21 April 1941, south-west of the Canary Islands, killing thirty-one crew. Seven men were killed when the first torpedo struck the engine-room and *Calchas* remained on an even keel, causing flooding to No. 6 hold. Captain Holden gave the order to abandon ship with a skeleton crew remaining on board. The captain of the submarine positioned her near *Calchas*'s lifeboats, which had been lowered into the water in an attempt to avoid being shelled. However, when the ship was hit by another torpedo, she sank with a loss of twenty-three of her crew.

Diomed (4) 1922 10,453 490.8x62.4x39.6 Steam Turbine 6,340 14 knots
B Workman, Clark & Company, Belfast, for the China Mutual Steam Navigation Company.
Calchas class. She gave thirty years service and arrived at Dalmuir on 2 September 1952 to be broken up by W. H. Arnott Young.

Above left: Diomed (4).

Above right: Perseus (2).

Left: Menelaus (3).

Perseus (2) 1923 10,286 490.5x62.3x39.6 Steam Turbine 6,336 14 knots
B Caledon Shipbuilding & Engineering Company, Dundee, for the China Mutual Steam Navigation Company.
Calchas class. On 16 January 1944, she was torpedoed off Madras by the Japanese submarine I-165 and all crew were saved.

Menelaus (3) 1923 10,278 490.5x53.0x39.6 Steam Turbine 6,334 14 knots
B Caledon Shipbuilding & Engineering Company, Dundee.
Delivered to the Ocean Steamship Company. Collided with *City of London* in 1940. On Christmas Day 1940, she was attacked by the German warship *Admiral Hipper* in the Mediterranean when escort vessels came to her rescue. On a voyage from Durban to Baltimore on 1 May 1942, she was attacked by the German Raider *Michel*, south-west of St Helena, but outran the vessel and escaped. The captain of the *Michel*, Hellmuth von Ruskteschell, credited with sinking over 168,000 tons of Allied shipping, is reported as saying, 'If you ever meet the captain of the Blue Funnel liner *Menelaus* give him my compliments. He was the only man who out-manoeuvred me and got away.' She arrived at Dalmuir on 25 June 1952 to be broken up.

Machaon (2) 1920 7,806 459.2x56.3x32.5 Steam Turbine 4,909 11 knots
B Caledon Shipbuilding & Engineering Company.
Delivered to the Ocean Steamship Company, transferred to the Glen Line in 1935, becoming *Glenaffaric*, and *Machaon* in 1947. Renamed *Glenaffaric* again for the Glen Line in 1950 and broken up at Briton Ferry by Thos.W.Ward in 1951.

Dardanus (3) 1923 7,823 459.5x58.4x32.6 Steam Turbine 4,920 11 knots
B Workman, Clark & Company, Belfast.
Machaon class. Delivered to the Ocean Steamship Company and transferred to Glen Line in 1935, becoming *Flintshire*, and *Dardanus* again in 1939. On 6 April 1942, she was bombed by a Japanese cruiser in the Indian Ocean and was taken in tow by British India Line's *Gandara*, but both were bombed and sunk the following day in the Bay of Bengal.

Glaucus (3).

Meriones.

Eumaeus (2) 1921 7,736 459.2x56.3x32.5 Steam Turbine 4,849 14 knots
B Caledon Shipbuilding & Engineering Company, Dundee.
On 14 January 1941, on a voyage from Liverpool to Cape Town, she was attacked by the Italian submarine Commandante Capellini, which fired shells hitting her stern and bridge. The submarine opened fire at 2,000 yards, closing to 1,000 yards and eventually to 700 yards. At least four direct hits were received on the bridge, but the steering continued to function, allowing the ship to avoid some of the gunfire. Captain J. E.Watson ordered full speed, and *Eumaeus* continued to return fire at the submarine until they ran out of shells. The vessel developed a heavy list to starboard and began to slow down. The engine-room crew were given the order to abandon ship when the ship started to settle by the head. On board were 400 naval ratings and her crew of ninety men. The ship was well ablaze and was abandoned when the submarine fired a torpedo and sank her. Twenty-three lives were lost.

Glaucus (3) 1921 7,644 459.5x56.3x32.5 Steam Turbine 4,849 14 knots
B Hawthorn, Leslie & Company, Newcastle.
Eumaeus class. The company stated at the time of her building that *Glaucus* had a specially designed raked stem to minimise the amount of damage in the event of a collision and also to give special protection to ropes. She was a two-deck type with poop, bridge and forecastle. On completion, she had accommodation on her bridge deck for first class passengers. While on convoy on 4 May 1943, she collided with the Shell tanker *Macuba* while avoiding Ellerman Line's *City of Florence*. It took five years for Shell to obtain damages for this incident. Along with five other Alfred Holt vessels, she took part in Operation *Husky*, the Sicily landings. She arrived at Bromborough Dock at Birkenhead on 26 July 1955 to be laid up and was sold to Thos. W. Ward later that year to be broken up at Milford Haven.

Meriones 1922 7,684 459.7x58.4x32.6 Steam Turbine 4,810 14 knots
B Hawthorn, Leslie & Company, Newcastle, for the China Mutual Steam Navigation Company.
Eumaeus class. On a voyage from London and Hull to Brisbane on 22 January 1941, she went aground on a wreck on the South Halsborough Bank, east of Cromer, and her crew were rescued by the Cromer lifeboat. The wreck was bombed by German aircraft, set on fire and sunk on 26 January.

Rhexenor 1922 7,957 459.6x58.3x32.6 Steam Turbine 5,004 14 knots
B Taikoo Dockyard & Engineering Company, Hong Kong.
Eumaeus class. Torpedoed by the German submarine U-217 on 3 February 1943 in the North Atlantic, south-east of Bermuda. She was on a voyage from Durban to British ports via Takoradi, Freetown and St John's. The crew abandoned the sinking vessel and were in the lifeboats for several weeks. The number 1 lifeboat reached Guadaloupe on 20 February, number 4 lifeboat reached Antigua the following day, number 3 lifeboat was sighted by an aircraft and the survivors were rescued by ship on 23 February, and number 5 lifeboat reached Jost van Goyen Island, Tobago, the same day.

Automedon.

Autolycus (2).

Automedon 1922 7,628 459.4x58.4x32.6 Steam Turbine 4,724 14 knots
B Palmers Shipbuilding & Iron Company, Jarrow.
Eumaeus class. On 11 November 1940, as she was sailing between the Nicobar Islands and Sri Lanka, she became aware that the German armed merchant cruiser *Atlantis* was in the area. When the two vessels came close to each other, the German captain fired a warning shot and the *Automedon* radioed for assistance. However, the *Atlantis* fired again at the Blue Funnel vessel, demolishing the bridge, killing everyone on it, including Captain W. B. Ewan. *Automedon* was hit eleven times but continued to steam at full speed away from *Atlantis*. Further gunfire from the German vessel killed the gunner and stopped *Automedon*. A party from *Atlantis* boarded the ship to find most of the charts and papers on the bridge had been destroyed. They discovered that *Automedon* was bound for Penang, Singapore, Hong Kong and Shanghai with aircraft, cars, machinery spares, steel and copper sheets, bicycles, uniforms, whisky, cigarettes, mail and sewing machines. Kapitan Bernhard Rogge of *Atlantis* decided to transfer as much of the cargo as possible to his ship as well as the eighty-seven crew and three passengers. The crew of *Automedon* assisted in the transfer of the passengers and their possessions and pointed out where the whisky and cigarettes were stored. *Atlantis*'s crew forced the safe to find the contents included some Admiralty documents and charts that could not be destroyed when the crew on the bridge were killed. It also contained the Merchant Navy Code and Deciphering Tables 7, 8 and 9, and when the mail bags were loaded, Rogge found letters for the Commander in Chief, Far East, which contained cabinet papers, Far East defence stratagies, and a review of the war situation in Europe. There were also maps of minefields, fleet cipher tables and other coded documents. Rogge initially attempted to tow *Automedon* out of the main shipping lane but this was not possible, and bombs were placed on the vessel, and she was blown up and sank.

Autolycus (2) 1923 7,718 459.7x58.3x32.5 Steam Turbine 4,859 14 knots
B Hawthorn, Leslie & Company, Newcastle, for the China Mutual Steam Navigation Company.
Eumaeus class. On a voyage from Calcutta and Durban to British ports on 6 April 1942, she was attacked and sunk by Japanese warships in the Bay of Bengal. Sixteen of her crew were killed, and the survivors landed on the coast of Orissa two days later.

Adrastus/Euryades (2) 1923 7,905 459.5x58.1x32.5 Steam Turbine 4,948 14 knots
B Scott's Shipbuilding & Engineering Company, Greenock.
Eumaeus class. When in service as a pilgrim carrier, she had her lifeboats paired one above the other. In June 1927, her captain hanged himself in his cabin as they approached Penang. Renamed *Euryades* in 1951 to allow the name to be given to a new vessel, and in 1954, she operated on the Pacific service from the United States to the Philippines and East Indies. Later that year, she was laid up in Holy Loch before being broken up at Faslane by Metal Industries, where she arrived on 10 August 1954.

Phemius (2).

Phemius (2) 1921 7,669 459.1x56.2x32.5 Steam Turbine 4,787 14 knots
B Scott's Shipbuilding & Engineering Company, Greenock.
Eumaeus class. On 14 May 1932, during a hurricane in the Caribbean, she lost her funnel but was able to sail to the port of Kingston, Jamaica. A temporary funnel was installed, and she sailed to Hong Kong for repairs, where a new funnel was fitted. When the ship eventually returned to the Mersey, the crew were given a civic reception by the Lord Mayor of Liverpool, but Captain Evans was reprimanded by Lawrence Holt for taking his ship into the path of a hurricane. He also had to forfeit £200 insurance that Blue Funnel made all captains lodge, as the company did not insure its vessels. However, on his retirement in 1944, Lawrence Holt returned the £200 to the captain. In 1942, she sailed between Port Said and Malta commanded by Captain J. L. W. Johnstone, and on 19 December 1943, she was torpedoed and sunk by U-515, south of Accra when twenty-three people were killed.

Troilus (3) 1921 7,648 459.1x56.2x32.5 Steam Turbine 4,774 14 knots
B Scott's Shipbuilding & Engineering Company, Greenock, for the China Mutual Steam Navigation Company.
Sister of *Phemius*. She was part of a convoy of six ships, which left the Clyde on 5 June 1942, named Operation *Harpoon*, with supplies to Malta. The convoy passed Gibraltar on the night of 11/12 June and was then escorted by a battleship, two aircraft carriers, two cruisers and eight destroyers. As they neared Malta, they were joined by another cruiser, nine destroyers, four minesweepers and six launches. Another convoy, named Operation *Vigorous*, had left Alexandria at the same time. When the air attacks started, the enemy aircraft came from all directions in formations of thirty to fifty. The gunners aboard the ships shot down thirty planes, which then dropped bombs onto the vessels. The *Tanimbar* was sunk, *Oran* struck a mine, leaving *Troilus* as the only undamaged ship. The next day, ships of the Italian Navy opened fire from long range, but the escort ships came to the rescue of the merchant vessels. In the following days, the convoy was attacked by submarines, and two more ships were sunk by air attack. As they came closer to Malta, enemy aircraft were dropping mines and two destroyers and a minesweeper were mined, and the New Zealand Shipping Company's *Orari* hit a mine, but managed to follow *Troilus* into the harbour. Eleven ships had left Alexandria with only six arriving safely at Malta. *Troilus* survived the war until 31 August 1944, when she was torpedoed and sunk by U-859 east of Socotra Island in the Indian Ocean on a voyage from Colombo to Aden and Liverpool, when twenty-four of her crew were lost. The survivors were rescued after five days in the lifeboats by HMS *Taff* and HMA *Nadder* and were taken to Aden.

Right: Brandenburg.

Far right: Hecuba (2).

Hecuba (2) 1901 7,540 430.0x54.3x39.6 Steam Turbine 4,811 10 knots
B Bremer Vulcan, Vegesack, Germany, for Norddeutscher Lloyd as *Brandenburg*.
She was bought from the British Government in 1922, who had acquired her as a war loss reparation, and she was renamed *Hecuba*. However, Alfred Holt's found that she was uneconomic to operate, but she found employment with the government again by carrying cavalry from Constantinople to Egypt in 1923. She was sold in 1924 to be broken up in Italy and was given the name *Ada* for the delivery voyage.

Sarpedon (4) 1923 11,321 499.0x62.3x34.9 Steam Turbine 6,921 15½ knots
B Cammell, Laird & Company, Birkenhead.
Built as the first in a class of four ships to accommodate 155 first class passengers and eighty crew after the British Government had asked shipping operators to provide more passenger facilities on cargo vessels. With a forecastle, bridge deck and poop, there were three overall decks – upper, main and lower – six holds and nine main bulkheads, the watertight doors in them being worked electrically from the bridge or by hand. Fireproof bulkheads were fitted within the centrecastle and between the decks above. No. 5 hold and 'tween decks were insulated. The 155 first class passengers were accommodated in one-, two- and three-berth rooms. The saloon was in the fore end of the centrecastle and was the full breadth of the ship, with pantries and galleys abaft of it. A lounge, smoking room and veranda café were provided on the promenade deck and a children's playground on the bridge deck. The engineer's accommodation was on the upper deck amidships, and the seamen and firemen in the poop. The master's and officers' accommodation was forward on the boat deck, where a separate house between the two hatchways aft of the bridge had a short boat deck above it with a small boat either side and two derrick posts with their standing derricks and electrical winches. There were fourteen steam and six electrical winches with twenty-four derricks, fourteen wooden and ten steel, plus a 20-ton derrick at the foremast. Thermotank ventilation and heating was fitted in all living spaces amidships. The passenger accommodation was described as thoroughly comfortable and homely, with plenty of space. Food was excellent, and being a one-class ship, passengers had the full run of the ship. Holt's described the accommodation as being more like that of a good country club at sea rather than a 'super' hotel.

On trials prior to her maiden voyage on 9 June 1923, she took relief supplies to the people of St Kilda, who were in distress, and food and other necessities were supplied by Holt's. During the Sino-Japanese War, she carried supplies and ammunition to Hong Kong. She survived the Second World War unscathed and took the first postwar sailing from Liverpool to Brisbane on 5 January 1946 with forty-eight passengers. She arrived at John Cashmore & Company in Newport, Monmouthshire, on 5 June 1953 to be broken up.

Patroclus (3) 1923 11,314 498.8x62.3x34.9 Steam Turbine 6,910 15½ knots
B Scott's Shipbuilding & Engineering Company, Greenock, for the China Mutual Steam Navigation Company.
Sarpedon class. She was requisitioned by the Admiralty in 1939 as an Armed Merchant Cruiser and was fitted with six 6-inch and two 3-inch guns at the aft

Sarpedon (4).

Patroclus (3).

end of the superstructure. The six 6-inch guns were carried on the forecastle, one on the poop, and two in each well deck. On 3 November 1940, she and the *Laurentic* were returning home from the Western patrol, and *Laurentic* went to the assistance of the *Casanare*. *Laurentic* was then torpedoed by U-99. The torpedo hit her in the engine-room and all power ceased. She was struck twice more by torpedoes and went down at the stern. *Patroclus* came to assist and dropped depth charges and attempted to rescue the crew from the water but was hit herself by a torpedo and at 22.55, she was hit by two further torpedoes. The submarine surfaced and fired at *Patroclus*, but when the fire was returned, the submarine submerged. *Patroclus* sank the following day after remaining afloat for over eight hours, and the crew were picked up by HMS *Achates*. However, seventy-six of the crew lost their lives. It has been reported that these Armed Merchant Cruisers required 2,600 tons of rock ballast and that their holds were filled with around 22,000 empty drums to keep them afloat when damaged. It is thought that this is why *Patroclus* remained afloat for so long after she was attacked.

Hector (4) 1924 11,198 498.8x62.3x34.9 Steam Turbine 6,481 15½ knots
B Scott's Shipbuilding & Engineering Company, Greenock.
Sarpedon class. She was converted to an Armed Merchant Cruiser in 1940, fitted with the same armaments as *Patroclus* and was sunk by a heavy Japanese air attack in Colombo Harbour on 5 April 1942. She was in the harbour decommissioning after over two years as an Armed Merchant Cruiser. Most of her crew were ashore, and she could not be got to sea, and she was struck by five heavy bombs, was badly holed and set on fire. The crew on board fought the fire for three hours and then were forced to abandon her with three forward holds flooded and gutted amidships. She was refloated in January 1946, later beached about five miles further up the coast, but was condemned and demolished where she lay.

Antenor (3) 1925 11,174 487.7x62.2x35.0 Steam Turbine 6,809 15½ knots
B Palmer's & Company, Jarrow.
Sarpedon class. In September 1937, she carried five giant pandas from Hong Kong to London. However, when they ate their wooden cage, they were placed in the potato lockers on the poop deck. She was requisitioned by the Admiralty in September 1939 becoming an Armed Merchant Cruiser, fitted with the same specification guns as *Patroclus* and converted to a troopship in 1942, becoming involved in the invasion of Normandy in 1944. She was returned to the Ocean Steamship Company in 1946 and survived until 1953, when she was broken up at Blyth by Hughes Bolckow.

Tantalus (2) 1923 7,777 458.3x58.2x32.6 Diesel 4,800 —
B Caledon Shipbuilding & Engineering Company, Dundee.
In 1936, she was transferred to the Glen Line and renamed *Radnorshire*, reverting back to Blue Funnel Line in 1939 as *Tantalus*. In 1941, she was undergoing a refit at Hong Kong when the Japanese attacked the colony. It was decided to tow her to Manila, arriving during a Japanese attack, and she was then moved to Bataan, where she was abandoned by her crew on Boxing Day as Japanese planes set her on fire. She capsized and sank, and when the Japanese took control of Manila, they captured two of *Tantalus*'s crew and executed them.

Medon 1923 5,915 406.5x52.2x29.3 Diesel 3,268 12 knots
B Palmer's & Company, Newcastle.
She was Alfred Holt's first motorship. On a voyage from Mauritius, Cape Town, and Trinidad to New York she was attacked by the Italian submarine Reginaldo Giuliano between Freetown and Trinidad on 10 August 1942. The submarine fired at her and sent a torpedo, which sustained a direct hit on *Medon*. The crew were able to take to the boats and later returned to collect possessions and other items before the submarine fired another torpedo and sank the vessel. The crew in number 4 lifeboat were adrift for seven days before they were rescued by *Tamerlane*, number 1 lifeboat crew were picked up by *Rosemount* eight days later, number 2 lifeboat was adrift for thirty-five days before they were rescued by the Portuguese vessel *Luso*, and number 3 lifeboat crew were finally picked up by the British vessel *Reedpool* after thirty-six days. The *Reedpool* was torpedoed by U-515 about 150 miles from Georgetown, British Guayana, on 20 September with thirty-four of her own crew and sixteen crew from *Medon*. The fifty survivors were able to get into a lifeboat and were rescued by the *Millie M. Masher* the following day.

Dolius 1924 5,994 406.5x52.2x28.4 Diesel/Steam 3,645 12 knots
B Scott's Shipbuilding & Engineering Company, Greenock.
The first Holt vessel to be fitted with part-steam and part-diesel engines, resulting in a saving in fuel and the installation of similar machinery in *Eurybates*. She was bombed by German aircraft on 24 April 1941 in the Firth of Forth and survived the attack. On a voyage from Avonmouth and Milford Haven to New York in convoy on 5 August 1943, she was torpedoed and sunk by U-638, east of Belle Isle in the Gulf of Lawrence. Survivors were rescued by HMS *Sunflower*, and U-638 was sunk by the convoy's escort vessels.

Eurymedon (2).

Eurymedon (2) 1924 6,223 431.8x54.7x30.1 Diesel 3,858 12 knots
B Caledon Shipbuilding & Engineering Company, Dundee.
The first of three similar vessels. On a voyage from Liverpool to Java via Cape Town, in convoy on 25 September 1940, she was attacked by U-29 and hit by two torpedoes in the North Atlantic. One torpedo hit the engine-room and the other holed the vessel and damaged a lifeboat that was being lowered, killing the passengers and crew. The following day, Captain J. F. Webster and crew went aboard but discovered that the ship could not be saved. Another lifeboat from Donaldson Line's *Sularia*, which had been sunk by U-43, took them off, and *Eurymedon* sank two days later. Twenty-eight lives were lost.

Polydorus 1924 6,256 429.9x54.8x30.1 Steam Turbine 3,863 12 knots
B Scott's Shipbuilding & Engineering Company, Greenock.
Eurymedon class. Managed by NSM 'Oceaan' as their first new ship. In Convoy ON-145 on a voyage from Liverpool to Freetown on 25 November 1942, she was attacked by the German submarine U-176. The submarine fired six torpedoes at *Polydorus*, which all missed her, but she was eventually damaged by gunfire from U-176. She sank two days later after two torpedoes were fired at her. The eighty survivors were rescued two days later by *Eolo*.

Melampus 1924 6,321 449.5x54.9x30.1 Steam Turbine 3,904 12 knots
B Palmer's & Company, Newcastle.
Sister to *Eurymedon*. Managed by NSM 'Oceaan' and her registry transferred to Willemstad in 1940 and came under the British flag in 1950. She was laid up in Holy Loch in 1955 and arrived at Inverkeithing on 1 October 1957 to be broken up by Thos. W. Ward.

Centaur (2) 1924 3,066 315.7x48.2x21.5 Diesel 1,800 14 knots
B Scott's Shipbuilding & Engineering Company, Greenock, for the Singapore to Australia service.
In 1940, she was converted to a hospital ship for the Australian Government, and on 14 May 1943, she was attacked by the Japanese submarine I-177 off Brisbane on a voyage from Sydney to New Guinea. The vessel was fully illuminated and was clearly marked as a hospital ship and sank in three minutes near Cape Moreton, off the Queensland coast, with the loss of 268 lives, including eighteen doctors and eleven nurses. Just one of the twelve nursing sisters on board survived. *Centaur* had been converted and repainted as a hospital ship with a green band 2 metres wide stretching around and with three red crosses painted on the white hull. A red cross was painted on the monkey island deck six metres by six metres and a larger red cross painted on the docking bridge aft and another hanging from the bridge aft. The lighting on the forward decks was turned off at night as it affected the vision of those on the bridge. At the end of the war, the captain of I-177 Lt-Cdr Hajime Nakagawa was arrested for war crimes and spent four years in prison for atrocities committed in the war. The wreck was declared a historic wreck in 1990.

Asphalion.

Asphalion 1924 6,274 431.7x54.7x30.1 Steam Turbine 3,836 12 knots
B Scott's Shipbuilding & engineering Company, Greenock, for the China Mutual Steam Navigation Company. She was the last coal burner built for Alfred Holt. On 11 February 1944, she was damaged by a torpedo off Vizagapatam in the Bay of Bengal and was towed to Calcutta for repairs to be carried out. Sold to Dah Cheong Hong Limited, of Hong Kong, to be broken up in 1959.

Alcinous (2)/Phemius (3) 1925 6,639 429.8x54.8x29.0 Diesel 4,131 14 knots
B Scott's Shipbuilding & Engineering Company, Greenock.
First of three sisters. Managed by NSM 'Oceaan' and renamed *Phemius* when transferred to the British registry in 1950. Arrived at Hong Kong on 26 July 1957 to be broken up.

Stentor (3) 1926 6,634 430.8x55.8x29.0 Diesel 4,161 14 knots
B Caledon Shipbuilding & engineering Company, Dundee, for the China Mutual Steam Navigation Company.
Alcinous class. Collided with and sank the Union Castle Line vessel *Guildford Castle* on 31 May 1933 with both vessels found to be to blame. On 16 September 1939, she collided with the British India vessel *Dilwari* while on a westbound Mediterranean convoy and was involved in a 'friendly fire' incident in Jeddah, when she was fired upon by British aircraft on 3 April 1941. On a voyage from Freetown to British ports on 27 October 1942 as part of a convoy, she was attacked by the German submarine U-509 west of the Canary Islands. She was lead ship in the convoy of forty vessels and sank in eight minutes after being hit by a torpedo. Captain Williams, twenty-one crew and twenty-three passengers died and Commodore Gastin, who was in charge of the convoy aboard *Stentor* also died. Survivors were picked up by HMS *Woodruff*.

Stentor (3).

Phrontis 1925 6,635 429.5x55.8x29.0 Diesel 4,136 14 knots
B Caledon Shipbuilding & Engineering Company, Dundee.
Alcinous class. Managed by NSM 'Oceaan' and sold to M. Bakhashab, Saudi Arabia, in 1958, becoming *Ryad*, and arrived at Hong Kong on 25 August that year to be broken up.

Peisander 1925 6,225 431.8x54.7x30.1 Diesel 3,884 12 knots
B Caledon Shipbuilding & Engineering Company, Dundee.
On a voyage from Newcastle, NSW, to Liverpool on 17 May 1942, she was torpedoed by the German submarine U-653 off Nantucket. Three lifeboats were successfully launched. Survivors in boat number 2 were rescued by the United States Coastguard vessel *General Green* and boats numbers 4 and 6 were found by the *Baron Semphill*, but as she was en route to South Africa, they declined and reached Nantucket Island four days later.

Prometheus (3) 1925 6,256 431.2x54.7x30.1 Diesel 3,872 12 knots
B Scott's Shipbuilding & Engineering Company, Greenock.
Peisander class. Attacked by enemy aircraft 270 miles off Rockall on 26 February 1941, and during 1942 and 1943, she took part in North Africa, Sicily and Salerno landings. Sold to Janus Compania de Nav. SA in 1957, renamed *Janus*, and laid up in Alicante the following year. In October that year, she caught fire at her berth and was towed out to sea, as there was a risk of a serious explosion. When the fire was extinquished, an inspection showed that it would be uneconomic to repair her and she was demolished in Italy in 1959.

Orestes (4) 1926 7,845 459.6x58.4x32.6 Diesel 4,809 14½ knots
B Workman, Clark & Company, Belfast.
Orestes and her sister *Idomeneus* were the highest-powered diesel-engine cargo ships afloat at the time. She was attacked by a Japanese seaplane off Madras in May 1942, which dropped four bombs that all missed *Orestes*. The following month, she was attacked by three Japanese submarines, 90 miles south of Sydney. *Orestes* was hit by two shells and the depth charges she dropped damaged one of the submarines, ending the attack. She survived the rest of the war, and in 1946, she was refurbished at Rotterdam. In 1954, her cargo of sisal

Above left: *Orestes* (4).

Above right: *Xanthus.*

Left: *Eurybates* (2).

caught fire at Walsh Bay, Sydney, and it took two days to extinquish the blaze. On 11 August 1963, she arrived at Mihara, Japan, to be broken up.

Idomeneus (2) 1926 7,857 459.6x58.4x32.6 Diesel 4,813 14½ knots
B Workman, Clark & Company, Belfast, for the China Mutual Steam Navigation Company.
Sister of *Orestes*. She was equipped with an insulated chamber, which chilled beef with a mixture of carbon dioxide and air, and as the system was successful, it was installed in other Holt vessels employed on the Australian service. On convoy off Cape Race on 21 November 1942, she had to change course to avoid the *British Promise*, which was directly ahead of her and had been torpedoed by U-518. *British Renown* and *Empire Sailor* were also torpedoed. The *British Promise* and *British Renown* later managed to reach Halifax but *Empire Sailor* sank with a loss of twenty-two crew, who died after inhaling fumes from her cargo of phosgene gas. This was the only incident in the Second World War involving the escape of a cargo of gas. On 7 May 1943, she avoided a torpedo that had been fired at her. She arrived at Genoa on 6 April 1962 to be broken up.

Xanthus 1927 213 102.8x22.7x10.1 Compound Steam 91 8 knots
B Cammell, Laird & Company, Birkenhead, as an oil separation barge for use on the River Mersey.
In 1959, she was sold to T. Routledge at Seaforth, renamed *Crosby Dale* and used as a tank barge. In June 1968, she was towed to Dalmuir by the Alexandra tug *Egerton* to be broken up by W. H. Arnott Young & Company.

Eurybates (2) 1928 6,436 431.9x54.8x29.1 Steam/Diesel 3,988 13½ knots
B Scott's Shipbuilding & Engineering Company, Greenock.
The experimental part-steam and part-diesel engines were not successful, and she was re-engined by Harland & Wolff in 1948, and the steam machinery was removed. She arrived at Ghent on 15 July 1958 to be broken up by Van Heyghen Freres.

Agamemnon (3) 1929 7,593 459.8x59.4x29.3 Diesel 4,806 14 knots
B Workman, Clark & Company, Belfast.
Built for the Liverpool to Far East route and also for the round-the-world service. Requisitioned by the Admiralty in 1939, becoming a minelayer as HMS *Agamemnon* with the First Minelayer Squadron. In 1943, she was converted into a Pacific fleet recreation ship at Vancouver to enable sailors to take their leave aboard her. She was fitted with a cinema/theatre, brewery and swimming pool. In March 1947, she returned to service and was broken up at Hong Kong in 1963.

Menestheus 1929 7,715 460.0x59.4x28.6 Diesel 4,796 14 knots
B Caledon Shipbuilding & Engineering Company, Dundee.
Agamemnon class. Requisitioned by the Admiralty in 1939 for use as a minesweeper and was bombed off Iceland in 1942 and was towed to Lochalsh to be repaired. In 1943, she was converted to a naval recreational ship and a second funnel was added to her. On 16 April 1953, she caught fire after an explosion in her engine-room off Punta Eugenio, California. She was abandoned and her crew were rescued by the *Navajo Victory*. The following day, her master and chief engineer boarded her and she was towed stern first to Magdelena Bay and later to Long Beach, where an enquiry was held to ascertain the cause of the fire. The board's findings were used to update the fire-safety regulations and equipment in Holt's vessels. She arrived at Baltimore in June 1953 to be broken up as Blue Funnel's first marine loss, excluding war losses, for thirty-six years.

Deucalion (3) 1930 7,740 460.0x59.4x29.3 Diesel 4,799 14 knots
B Hawthorn, Leslie & Company, Newcastle.
Agamemnon class. She was bombed and damaged in Gladstone Dock, Liverpool, during an air raid on 21/22 December 1940. As she was leaving Malta in July the following year, she was fired upon by shore batteries and a mine was set off. The same day, she was attacked by Italian Marchetti bombers, whose torpedoes scraped the side of the ship. One of the Italian aircraft was shot down and a submarine periscope was seen briefly until an escorting destroyer arrived on the scene. On 12 August 1942, she was attacked and sunk by an air attack west of Cani Rocks, Gallita Island, on a voyage in a convoy to Malta known as Operation *Pedestal*. She was the leading cargo ship, which was targeted by a German fighter aircraft, which dropped four bombs on her. Three bombs missed but the fourth went through number 5 hold and through the side of the ship. With the vessel severely damaged, Captain Ramsay Brown attempted to maintain her course until three enemy aircraft found her and an aerial torpedo exploded in number 6 hold breaking the propeller shaft and igniting the cargo of high-octane fuel. The captain gave the order to abandon ship. Midshipmen J. S. Gregory and P. T. Bracewell helped a naval gunner who was wounded to the side of the ship and towed him to safety, which earned Gregory the Albert Medal, the highest civilian award for gallantry. Survivors were taken aboard HMS *Branham*, which fired two depth charges, sinking *Deucalion*.

Memnon (4) 1931 7,731 460.0x59.4x29.3 Diesel 4,765 14 knots
B Caledon Shipbuilding & Engineering Company, Greenock for the China Mutual Steam Navigation Company.
Sister to *Agamemnon*. Torpedoed and sunk in 15 minutes by U-106, north-east of Cape Blanco, Cape Verde Islands, on a voyage from Port Pirie, Freetown, to Swansea and Avonmouth on 11 March 1941.

Ajax (3)/Sarpedon (5) 1931 7,797 459.6x59.3x29.2 Diesel 4,803 14 knots
B Scott's Shipbuilding & Engineering Company, Greenock.
Delivered to the Ocean Steamship Company, transferred to Glen Line in 1957 and renamed *Glenlochy*, and *Sarpedon* the following year. She arrived at Hong Kong to be broken up in 1962.

Maron 1930 6,701 433.0x56.3x26.3 Diesel 4,114 13½ knots
B Caledon Shipbuilding & Engineering Company, Dundee, for the China Mutual Steam Navigation Company.

Ajax (3).

Maron.

The first of a class of four ships. On 12 August 1937, she carried 1,100 Royal Welsh Fusiliers from Hong Kong to Shanghai and evacuated British expatriates from the threat of Japanese advancement. She was also requisitioned by the Admiralty in 1939 and was torpedoed and sunk on 13 November 1942 by U-81 in the Mediterranean off Oran on a voyage from Algiers to Gibraltar. Survivors were rescued by HMS *Marigold* and were taken to Gibraltar.

Clytoneus 1930 6,663 432.5x56.3x26.3 Diesel 4,110 13½ knots
B Scott's Shipbuilding & Engineering Company, Greenock.
Maron class. On 8 January 1941, on a voyage from Macassar to Ellesmere Port via Belewan, Cape Town and Freetown, under command of Captain S. G. Goffey, she was attacked by enemy aircraft off Ireland. Two near misses stopped the main engine, and the second low-level attack set fire to the cargo of sugar, tea, kapok, and flour in number 2 hold. *Clytoneus* began to sink after the attack, which only lasted 8 minutes, and after abandoning ship, the survivors were rescued by HMS *Wild Swan* and the *Esperance Bay*.

Myrmidon (3) 1930 6,663 432.5x56.3x26.3 Diesel 4,110 13½ knots
B Scott's Shipbuilding & Engineering Company.
Maron class. While berthed at Birkenhead on 13 April 1941, a parachute mine exploded near her, and when she was towed away from the berth, another mine exploded, causing her to sink. Following salvage, she was raised and repaired, and after she left Birkenhead on 5 June, she struck another mine. Repairs took six months to complete. On 5 September the following year, on a voyage from Glasgow to Freetown, Cape Town, Bombay and Colombo, she was torpedoed and sunk by U-506 off Cape Palmas, Liberia.

Polyphemus (3) 1930 6,671 430.5x56.3x26.3 Diesel 4,117 13½ knots
B Scott's Shipbuilding & Engineering Company, Greenock.
Maron class. Managed by NSM 'Oceaan'. On 22 November 1941, the German Armed Merchant Cruiser *Atlantis*, commanded by Kapitan Bernhard Rogge, was detected by HMS *Devonshire* between the Ascension Isles and Freetown. *Atlantis* sent out a signal, 'RRR *Polyphemus*', saying that *Polyphemus* was being attacked. Captain R. D. Oliver of HMS *Devonshire* detected that the message did not comply with the correct code, but as *Polyphemus* had been in the area, it could be a genuine call for assistance. He then sent the Walrus aircraft to *Atlantis* to clarify which vessel it was, and when he realised it was not *Polyphemus*, he opened fire and sank *Atlantis* after the crew scuttled her and abandoned ship. On 26 May 1942, on a voyage from Sydney to Halifax and Liverpool, she was torpedoed twice and sank, north of Bermuda. *Polyphemus* was carrying fourteen survivors from the *Norland*, and out of seventy-four people aboard, only thirty survived.

Gorgon (2) 1933 3,533 320.3x51.2x21.6 Diesel 2,120 12 knots
B Caledon Shipbuilding & Engineering Company, Dundee, for the joint service with the West Australian Steam Navigation Company (Bethell, Gwynn & Company) between Singapore and West Australian ports.
She was wholly owned by the Ocean Steamship Company in 1936. On 3 February 1942, she sailed from Singapore with 300 passengers aboard, which was three days before the surrender to Japanese forces, and she was attacked by Japanese bombers on six occasions, and the ship was set alight next to the ammunition store. An unexploded bomb was found in bags of flour, which was dropped over the side of the ship, and the blaze was brought under control. She was bombed again on 14 April the following year in Milne Bay, New Guinea, when six of her crew were killed and the ship set on fire. The damage was so extensive that *Gorgon* had to be towed back to Brisbane to be repaired. She returned to service at the end of the war and took her last sailing from Fremantle on 21 July 1964 and was sold for breaking up at Hong Kong.

Charon (2) 1936 3,703 320.3x51.2x21.6 Diesel 2,217 12 knots
B Caledon Shipbuilding & Engineering Company, Dundee, for the same service.
Sister of *Gorgon*. She also became fully owned by the Ocean Steamship Company in 1936. She kept the Australian base at Milne Bay supplied in 1943,

Gorgon (2).

Charon (2).

completing thirty voyages between Sydney and New Guinea without incident. Sold in 1964 to shipbreakers at Singapore, who resold her to Chan Kai Kit of Panama, becoming *Seng Kong* No. 1. She was broken up the following year.

Jason (3) 1940 6,130 449.5x60.9x25.9 Diesel — —
B Cantieri Riuniti dell Adriatico, Monfalcone.
She was laid down for Lloyd Triestino and bought on the stocks by NSM 'Oceaan' and her trials on 9 May 1940 were carried out under the Dutch flag. However, Holland was attacked by Germany that day and the Italian Government decided that she could not be delivered and renamed her *Sebastiano Veniero*, operated by Societa Italiano di Armamento. Italy entered the Second World War a month later on 10 June. The NSM 'Oceaan' crew were brought back to Britain by *Perseus*. *Sebastiano Veniero* came under the German Mittelmeer Reederei GmbH (Mediterranean Steamship Company) and was torpedoed by HMS *Torbay* and HMS *Porpoise* on 9 December 1941, south of Navarino, and was beached and later declared a total loss. Technically, she had been a member of the fleet for one day.

Priam (4)/Phemius (4) 1941 9,975 486.1x66.4x32.3 Diesel 5,944 —
B Caledon Shipbuilding & Engineering Company, Dundee.
She was requisitioned by the Admiralty while she was on the stocks. It was decided to complete the vessel to her original specifications, and she was returned to Alfred Holt's and completed as *Priam*. Transferred to the Glen Line in 1948, becoming *Glenorchy*, and back to Blue Funnel in 1970, renamed *Phemius*. She was broken up at Kaohsiung, Taiwan, the following year.

Telemachus (3) 1943 9,061 486.1.x65.2x32.3 Diesel 5,314 —
B Caledon Shipbuilding & Engineering Company.
Sister to *Priam*. Her keel was laid on 1 February 1940, and she was requisitioned by the Admiralty while on the stocks and given the name *Empire Activity*. As it was economically feasible to alter her plans, she was built as an escort carrier and was delivered as HMS *Activity*. She operated as a deck-landing training ship with fifteen aircraft and two 4-inch guns with a crew of 700, and also escorted Atlantic and Arctic convoys. She was working in the Arctic in 1944 with HMS *Avenger* and HMS *Tracker*, sinking three U-boats. The following year, she was transferred to the Far East to transport aircraft to the British Pacific fleets and later carried aircraft parts and supplies to Sri Lanka. She was sold to the Glen Line in 1946 and sent to Palmer's at Hebburn to be converted back to her original design and renamed *Breconshire*. She was handed over on 12 September 1947 and gave the line twenty years of service, as she was broken up at Kobe in 1967. Consequently, *Telemachus* did not actually sail for Blue Funnel.

Telemachus (4)/Glaucus (4) 1943 8,265 462.2x61.4x31.9 Diesel 4,817 —
Transferred to the Glen Line in 1957, renamed *Monmouthshire* and back to the Ocean Steamship Company in 1963 as *Glaucus*. Renamed *Nanchang* on

charter to the China Navigation Company in 1964 and broken up in Hong Kong four years later.

Rhexenor (2) 1945 10,199 475.8x64.4x40.0 Diesel 6,022 15 knots
B Caledon Shipbuilding & Engineering Company, Dundee, for the China Mutual Steam Navigation Company.
She was laid down for the Ministry of War as an *Empire* vessel and taken over on the stocks by Blue Funnel. She operated on the Australian service, as she had a large refrigerated capacity, and as she had been designed to carry heavy loads, she also carried railway engines. In 1975, she was sold to be broken up at Kaohisung and she sailed there as *Hexeno*.

Stentor (4) 1946 10,203 475.8x64.4x40.0 Diesel 6,053 15 knots
B Caledon Shipbuilding & Engineering Company, Dundee.
Rhexenor class. She was also purchased on the stocks and completed for the Ocean Steamship Company. Transferred to the Glen Line in 1958 and renamed *Glenshiel*, and to the China Mutual Steam Navigation Company in 1963 as *Stentor*. In 1974, she operated on Elder Dempster routes and was sold in Singapore the following year to be broken up at Taiwan and sailed there as the *Tento*.

Medon (2) 1942 7,376 431.4x57.3x33.6 Diesel 4,408 12 knots
B Harland & Wolff, Belfast, for the Ministry of War Transport (G. Heyn & Sons as managers) as *Empire Splendour*.
Purchased by Blue Funnel Line in 1946 and renamed *Medon*. She was laid up in the River Fal in 1962 and sold to Olistim Nav. Cia of Monrovia the following year, becoming *Tina*. Purchased by Sanspyridon Shipping Company, Cyprus, in 1968 and broken up in 1970.

Calchas (3) 1947 7639 462.9x62.3x31.7 Diesel 4,526 15½ knots
B Harland & Wolff, Belfast.
First of a class of twenty-one vessels. Launched by Mrs Lawrence Holt on 27 August 1946 and known as the *Anchises* class Mark A1. She was the first vessel in Holt's postwar rebuilding programme and was delivered ahead of *Anchises* and owned by the China Mutual Steam Navigation Company. She was used as the company's training ship up to 1956 with twenty-two midshipmen cadets and fourteen engineering cadets. Transferred to the Glen Line in 1957, becoming *Glenfinlas*, and *Calchas* in 1962, operating for Elder Dempster Lines in 1971-72. In July 1973, she was severely damaged by a fire in Port Kelang, which took five days to extinguish, and it was found not to be economically viable to repair her. She was sold for breaking up in Kaohsiung, where she arrived by tow on 23 October.

Anchises (4)/Alcinous 1947 7,642 462.9x62.3x31.7 Diesel 4,474 15½ knots
B Caledon Shipbuilding & Engineering Company, Dundee.
Sister of *Calchas*. On a voyage from Woosung to Shanghai on the Wangpoo River on 21 June 1949, she was bombed by Chinese Nationalist fighter aircraft. Her engine-room was flooded and she sank in shallow water. She was refloated and towed to her berth to discharge, where she was bombed again, and was towed to Kobe in Japan to be repaired. In 1973, she was transferred to NSM 'Oceaan' and renamed *Alcinous*, transferred to the Glen Line in 1974 and to the China Mutual Steam Navigation Company later that year. She arrived at Kaohsiung on 5 September 1975 to be broken up.

Aeneas (2) 1947 7,641 462.9x62.3x31.7 Diesel 4,473 15½ knots
B Caledon Shipbuilding & Engineering Company, Dundee.
Sister of *Calchas*. Completed for the China Mutual Steam Navigation Company. She was broken up at Taiwan in 1972.

Agapenor (2) 1947 7,664 463.0x62.3x31.7 Diesel 4,460 15½ knots
B Scott's Shipbuilding & Engineering Company, Greenock, for the China Mutual Steam Navigation Company.
Sister of *Calchas*. In June 1967, she was trapped in the Suez Canal during the Israeli and Egypt Six-Day War. She was abandoned, becoming the property of Agapenor War Risks Limited, the Liverpool & London War Risks Insurance

Stentor (4).

Above left: *Calchas* (3).

Above right: *Anchises* (4).

Right: *Agapenor* (2).

Polyphemus (5).

Clytoneus (2) at Avonmouth.

Association. On 20 May 1975, she was towed to Port Said and then to Dhekelia in Cyprus, where ammunition was unloaded. She then went to Trieste to unload the rest of the cargo and was sold to the Grecomar Shipping Agency Limited and renamed *Nikos*, operated by the Faynav Shipping Company of Panama. She arrived at Piraeus to be overhauled on 27 July and was sold to be broken up in 1981.

Achilles (4)/Asphalion (2)/Polyphemus (5)/Asphalion
1948 7,632 462.9x62.3x31.7 Diesel 4,449 15½ knots
B Caledon Shipbuilding & Engineering Company, Dundee.
Sister of *Calchas*. Delivered to the Ocean Steamship Company and transferred to the Glen Line in 1949, becoming *Radnorshire*. She came under the Blue Funnel fleet again in 1962 and was renamed *Asphalion*. In 1966, she was transferred to NSM 'Oceaan' as *Polyphemus* and back to the Ocean Steamship Company in 1972 as *Asphalion*. Sold to Gulf (Shipowners) Limited, London, three years later, renamed *Gulf Anchor* and was broken up at Kaohsiung in 1979.

Astyanax (2) 1948 7,654 463.0x62.3x31.7 Diesel 4,481 15½ knots
B Scott's Shipbuilding & Engineering Company, Greenock, for the China Mutual Steam Navigation Company.
Sister of *Calchas*.
Transferred to the Glen Line in 1957, renamed *Glenfruin* and back to the Blue Funnel Line in 1962 as *Astyanax*. Broken up in Kaohsiung in 1972.

Clytoneus (2) 1948 7,620 462.9x62.3x31.7 Diesel 4,434 15½ knots
B Caledon Shipbuilding & Engineering Company, Dundee.
Sister of *Calchas*. Delivered in August 1948 as the first of the Mark A2 class of six ships, with 'tween deck accommodation for Far East pilgrims to Jeddah. They were built with wooden decks, portholes, extra ventilators, and sanitary and kitchen facilities. Lifeboats were doubled on top of each other. In 1971, she operated for Elder Dempster Lines and was broken up at Kaohsiung in 1972.

Cyclops (3)/Automedon (3) 1948 7,632 463.0x62.3x31.7 Diesel 4,476 15½ knots
B Scott's Shipbuilding & Engineering Company, Greenock.
Sister of *Calchas*. In September 1955, on a voyage from Liverpool to Kobe, she collided with the Henderson Line's *Prome*, south-west of Holyhead, and had to return to Liverpool for survey and repairs. In 1975, she had her radar fitted to the funnel top to improve the range, and in July that year, she was renamed *Automedon*, and transferred to Elder Dempster Lines. She was chartered to the Nigerian National Line in 1977 and arrived at Dalmuir in August that year to be broken up.

Autolycus (3) 1949 7,635 462.9x62.3x31.7 Diesel 4,438 15½ knots
B Harland & Wolff, Belfast, for the China Mutual Steam Navigation Company.
Sister of *Calchas*. Transferred to Elder Dempster Lines in 1974 and laid up at Bromborough Dock in June the following year and chartered to the Nigerian

Above: *Autolycus* (3).

Right: *Automedon* (2).

National Line in October that year. She was sold to Gulf (Shipowners) Limited of London in 1976, becoming *Gulf Trader* and chartered by them to the Nigerian National Line. She arrived at Taiwan two years later to be broken up.

Antilochus (2) 1949 7,635 462.9x62.3x31.7 Diesel 4,479 15½ knots
B Harland & Wolff, Belfast.
Sister of *Calchas*. Transferred to Elder Dempster Lines in 1975 and sold to Gulf (Shipowners) Limited of London two years later, becoming *Gulf Orient*. She arrived at Gadani Beach on 9 May 1978 to be broken up.

Automedon (2) 1949 7,636 462.9x62.3x31.7 Diesel 4,439 15½ knots
B Vickers Armstrong Limited, Newcastle.
Sister of *Calchas*. On 17 December 1971, she collided with the Greek vessel *San George* in the River Scheldt, and following a survey on the Tyne, it was found that it was not economic to repair her, and she was sold for scrap and arrived in Kaohsiung in March the following year.

Laertes (4)/Idomeneus (3) 1950 7,664 462.9x62.3x31.7 Diesel 4,533 15½ knots
B Vickers Armstrong Limited, Newcastle.
Sister of *Calchas*. Delivered in October 1950 as the final Mark A2-class vessel and managed by NSM 'Oceaan'. She was transferred to Blue Funnel in 1972, becoming *Idomeneus*, and was operated by Elder Dempster in 1975. Sold to Gulf Shipping Lines the following year, renamed *Gulf Voyager*, and arrived at Gadani Beach on 8 May 1978 to be broken up by Al Noor Steel Limited.

Above left: Obhor ex-*Bellerophon* (3).

Above right: Akosombo ex-*Ascanius* (2). (Victor Young)

Left: Atreus (2).

Bellerophon (3) 1950 7,707 462.9x62.3x31.7 Diesel 4,485 15½ knots
B Caledon Shipbuilding & Engineering Company, Dundee, as a Mark A3 vessel.
Sister of *Calchas*. Transferred to the Glen Line in 1957 and renamed *Cardiganshire* and back to the China Mutual Steam Navigation Company that year as *Bellerophon*. In 1975, she was operating for Elder Dempster Lines and was sold to Saudi-Europe Line Limited the following year, becoming *Obhor*. Two years later, she was chartered to make a film, and on conclusion of the charter, she was sold to be broken up at Gadani Beach, where she arrived on 23 September 1978.

Ascanius (2) 1950 7,692 462.9x62.3x31.7 Diesel 4,545 15½ knots
B Harland & Wolff, Belfast.
Sister of *Calchas*. Transferred to Elder Dempster Lines in 1972, and renamed *Akosombo*, and to the China Mutual Steam Navigation Company the following year as *Ascanius*. Sold to Saudi-Europe Line Limited in 1976 and renamed *Mastura*. She arrived at Blyth on 4 April 1978 to be broken up by Hughes Bolckow Limited.

Atreus (2) 1951 7,800 462.9x62.3x31.7 Diesel 4,545 15½ knots
B Vickers Armstrong Limited, Newcastle, for the China Mutual Steam Navigation Company.
Sister of *Calchas*. Sold to Sherwood Shipping Company, Singapore, in 1977 and renamed *United Valiant*. She arrived at Kaohsiung on 23 February 1979 to be broken up.

Alcinous (3)/Polydorus (3) 1952 7,799 487.2x62.3x31.7 Diesel 4,538 15½ knots
B Vickers Armstrong Limited, Newcastle, with the original intention to call her *Cadmus*.
Sister of *Calchas*. In 1960, she was transferred to NSM 'Oceaan', becoming *Polydorus*, and back to Blue Funnel in 1973. A new radar mast was also fitted in 1973. She was renamed *Johara* and sold to S. H. Alatas & Company in 1976, who

were the agents at the Port of Jeddah. As priority was given to local vessels in this port, this was a way of avoiding delays in loading and unloading. However, in November 1976, she was transferred to Elder Dempster ownership and sold to Hesperus Navigation Corporation of Monrovia in 1977 and renamed *Matina*. She arrived at Gadani Beach to be broken up on 23 April 1978.

Laomedon (2) 1953 7,864 487.2x62.3x31.7 Diesel 4,580 15½ knots
B Vickers Armstrong Limited, Newcastle for the China Mutual Steam Navigation Company.
Sister of *Calchas*. She gave the company twenty-four years service and was sold to Regent Navigation Corporation of Panama with the Maldives Shipping as managers and renamed *Aspasia*. On 20 April 1978, she left Kuwait to be broken up at Gadani Beach.

Eumaeus (4) 1953 7,681 462.9x62.3x31.7 Diesel 4,566 15½ knots
B Caledon Shipbuilding & Engineering Company, Dundee.
Sister of *Calchas*. She was the first of four Mark A4-class ships that had a poop hatch in place of a poop locker with the derrick posts positioned further forward. In 1962, she was transferred to NSM 'Oceaan' and arrived at Kaohsiung on 31 January 1978 to be broken up.

Adrastus (2) 1953 7,859 462.9x62.3x31.7 Diesel 4,573 15½ knots
B Vickers Armstrong Limited, Newcastle.
Sister of *Calchas*. Delivered in 1953 and transferred to NSM 'Oceaan' in 1961, spending a brief period in 1974 operating for Elder Dempster Lines and to the China Mutual Steam Navigation in 1975. Sold to Rhodeswell Shipping Company SA, Limassol, in 1978, becoming *Anassa*, and broken up at Gadani Beach in 1981. She was the last of the *Anchises* class to be broken up.

Elpenor (2) 1954 7,757 462.9x62.3x31.7 Diesel 4,509 15½ knots
B Harland & Wolff, Belfast, for the China Mutual Steam Navigation Company.
Sister of *Calchas*. She was sold in 1978 to the Cremorne Bay Shipping Company, Liberia, and renamed *United Concord*. She was broken up at Kaohsiung the following year.

Lycaon (2)/Glaucus (6) 1954 7,859 462.9x62.3x31.7 Diesel 4,567 15½ knots
B Vickers, Armstrong & Company, Newcastle, for the China Mutual Steam Navigation Company.
Sister of *Calchas*. Transferred to NSM 'Oceaan' in 1960 and to the Elder Dempster Lines under British registry in 1975. In December 1977, she was renamed *Glaucus* and was sold later that year to Marlborough Maritime Incorporated, Monrovia, and renamed *United Vanguard*. On 12 May 1979, on a voyage from Sharjah to Bassein, she suffered a serious engine failure and a ruptured sea-water cooling pipe and was abandoned with the loss of one member of crew. She sank the following day.

Polydorus (2)/ Talthybius (3) 1944 7,671 439.1x62.1x34.5 Steam Turbine 4,567 15 knots
B Permanente Metals Corporation, Richmond, California.

Polydorus (3).

Adrastus (2).

Tantalus (4).

Maron (2).

Built as *Salina Victory* and purchased by the Blue Funnel Line in 1946, operated by NSM 'Oceaan' and renamed *Polydorus*. She was transferred to the Ocean Steamship Company in 1960, renamed *Talthybius* and operated on Elder Dempster Lines services to West Africa in 1971 prior to being laid up at Bromborough Dock and sold for breaking up at Taiwan.

Polyphemus (4)/ Tantalus (4) 1945 7,674 439.1x62.1x34.5 Steam Turbine 4,562 15 knots
B Permanente Metals Corporation, Richmond, California.
Sister to *Polydorus*. Built as Mac Murray Victory and purchased by Alfred Holt in 1946, operated by NSM 'Oceaan' as Polyphemus. Transferred to the Ocean Steamship Company in 1960 and renamed *Tantalus*. She was laid up in the River Fal in March 1969 and sold later that year to be broken up at Taiwan and was renamed *Pelops* for the delivery voyage.

Maron (2)/Rhesus (2) 1945 7,713 439.1x62.1x34.5 Steam Turbine 4,546 15 knots
B Permanente Metals Corporation, Richmond, California.
Sister to *Polydorus*. Built as *Berywn Victory* for the United States Maritime Commission and purchased by the China Mutual Steam Navigation Company in 1947, becoming *Maron*. She was renamed *Rhesus* in 1957 and laid up three years later. Sold in 1962 to Overseas Maritime Company Incorporated of Monrovia, renamed *Pacific Telstar*, and arrived at Kaohsiung on 1 February 1974 to be broken up.

Mentor (2) 1945 7,642 439.1x62.1x34.5 Steam Turbine 4,537 15 knots
B Permanente Metals Corporation, Richmond, California.
Sister to *Polydorus*. Built as *Carthage Victory* and purchased by the Ocean Steamship Company in 1947 and renamed *Mentor*. She was sold in 1967 to Seawave Navigation Corporation of Greece, becoming *Vita*, *Viva* in 1969, *Syra* in 1971 and broken up at Split in 1971.

Memnon (5)/ Glaucus (5) 1945 7,711 439.1x62.1x34.5 Steam Turbine 4,567 15 knots
B Permanente Metals Corporation, Richmond, California.
Sister to *Polydorus*. Completed as *Phillips Victory* and purchased by the Ocean Steamship Company in 1946, renamed *Memnon*, and *Glaucus* in 1957. She was sold in 1962 to Iranian Lloyd Company Limited of Khorramsshar, becoming *Persian Ferdowsi*, and sold again the following year to Paul J. Frangoulis and A. & I. Cliafas of Piraeus and renamed *Eleni K*. However, she was arrested by Iran for unpaid debts in October 1966 and detained at Bandar Shapur for thirty-eight days. When released, she sailed and was re-arrested at sea by an Iranian destroyer, five frigates, three launches and a helicopter. In 1968, she was renamed *Pirouzi* but did not sail until May the following year, when she was towed to Hong Kong to be broken up.

Myrmidon (4) 1945 7,715 439.1x62.1x34.5 Steam Turbine 4,569 15 knots
B Permanente Metals Corporation, Richmond, California.

Mentor (2).

Euryades (3).

Sister to *Polydorus*. Built as *Ripon Victory* and purchased by the China Mutual Steam Navigation Company in 1947, becoming *Myrmidon*. She operated on their services until she was sold to be broken up by Tien Cheng Steel Manufacturing Company at Kaohsiung in 1971.

Eumaeus (3)/ Euryades (3) 1943 7,308 423.5x57.0x34.8 Triple Expansion 4,379 11 knots
B Bethlehem Fairfield Shipyard, Baltimore, Maryland.
Launched as *Simon B. Elliott* and completed as *Samnesse* for the Ministry of War, managed by Alfred Holt. She was purchased in 1947, becoming *Eumaeus*, owned by the China Mutual Steam Navigation Company, and transferred to the Glen Line in 1952, renamed *Glenshiel*. She was back with Blue Funnel in 1957 as *Euryades*, managed by the China Mutual Steam Navigation Company. Sold in 1961 to Bounty Shipping Company, Hong Kong, becoming *Marine Bounty*. On 25 February 1966, she went aground at Hasieshan in China. She was refloated but was soon aground again, abandoned and broke in two. She was on a voyage from Chingwantao to Singapore.

Eurymedon (3) 1943 7,314 423.5x57.0x34.8 Triple Expansion 4,405 11 knots
B Worthington Pump & Machinery Company, Harrison, New Jersey.
Sister of *Eumaeus*. Launched as *Matthew Brush* and completed as *Samoa* for the Ministry of War, managed by Alfred Holt. Purchased by the China Mutual Steam Navigation Company in 1947 and renamed *Eurymedon*. She was transferred to the Glen Line in 1952, becoming *Glenlogan*, and to the Blue Funnel Line in 1957 as *Eurymedon*. Sold to Etolika Cia Nav. SA of Piraeus the following year, becoming *Angelos*. In 1964, she was renamed *Mimosa* when sold to Michael A. Araktingi of Lebanon, Alplata, in 1966, owned by Alplata Shipping Corporation of Monrovia and Anka when purchased by Maria de Lourdes Shipping Company of Cyprus in 1967. She arrived at Bilbao on 25 June 1971 to be broken up.

Eurypylus (2) 1943 7,292 423.5x57.0x34.8 Triple Expansion 4,380 11 knots
B Worthington Pump & Machinery Company, Harrison, New Jersey.
Sister to *Eumaeus*. Launched as *Augustine Herman* and renamed *Samsette* when transferred to the Ministry of War, managed by Alfred Holt. Purchased by the China Mutual Steam Navigation Company in 1947 and renamed *Eurypylus*. Transferred to the Glen Line in 1950, becoming *Pembrokeshire*, and back to the Blue Funnel Line in 1957 as *Eurypylus*. Sold to the Federal Shipping Company of Hong Kong in 1960 and renamed *Kota Bahru*, and *Cresta* in 1966, when owned by Cresta Shipping Company Incorporated of Panama. She was broken up at Kaohsiung in 1968.

Troilus (4) 1943 7,287 441.7x57.0x34.8 Triple Expansion 4,375 11 knots
B Worthington Pump & Machinery Company, Harrison, New Jersey.
Sister to *Eumaeus*. Launched as *Martha C. Thomas*, becoming *Samharle* when transferred to the Ministry of War, managed by Alfred Holt & Company.

Purchased by the Ocean Steamship Company in 1947 and renamed *Troilus*. Sold to Cia de Nav. San Agustin SA in 1958, becoming *Green River*, and broken up at Osaka in 1963.

Tydeus (2) 1944 7,234 423.5x57.0x34.8 Triple Expansion 4,345 11 knots
B Worthington Pump & Machinery Company, Harrison, New Jersey.
Sister to *Eumaeus*. Delivered as *Samjack* to the Ministry of War, with Alfred Holt & Company as managers. Purchased by the Blue Funnel Line in 1947 and renamed *Tydeus*, transferred to the Glen Line in 1950 as *Glenbeg*. Sold to Foreman Shipping & Trading Incorporated in 1958, renamed *Roan*, and *Jucar* in 1960, owned by West African Carriers Corporation. She was broken up at Mihara in Japan in 1967.

Talthybius (2) 1943 7,291 423.5x57.0x34.8 Triple Expansion 4,380 11 knots
B Worthington Pump & Machinery Corporation, Harrison, New Jersey.
Sister to *Eumaeus*. Launched as *Peter Cooper* and transferred to the Ministry of War as *Samarkand*, managed by Alfred Holt & Company. Purchased by the Ocean Steamship Company in 1947, renamed *Talthybius*, transferred to Glen Line as *Gleniffer* in 1954 and sold to Colombine Shipping Company in 1958, becoming *Dove* and *Patraic Sky* in 1965, owned by Patriarch Steamship Company. She was broken up at Split in 1971.

Tantalus (3) 1943 7,297 423.9x57.0x34.8 Triple Expansion 4,385 11 knots
B Worthington Pump & Machinery Corporation, Harrison, New Jersey.
Sister to *Eumaeus*. Launched as *John T. Clark* and renamed *Samcleve* when transferred to the Ministry of War, managed by Alfred Holt & Company. Purchased by the Ocean Steamship Company in 1947, becoming *Tantalus*. Sold to Ditta Luigi Pittaluga Vapori of Genoa in 1958 and renamed *Urbania*, and *Cocler* in 1965, owned by Henry Coe and Clerici SPA. She was broken up in 1975.

Titan (3) 1943 7,297 423.9x57.0x34.8 Triple Expansion 4,385 11 knots
B Worthington Pump & Machinery Corporation, Harrison, New Jersey.
Sister to *Eumaeus*. Launched as *James Carroll* and renamed *Samgara* for the Ministry of War, managed by Alfred Holt & Company. Bought by the Ocean Steamship Company in 1947 and renamed *Titan*, transferred to the Glen Line in 1950 as *Flintshire*, and back to the Ocean Steamship Company in 1958 as *Titan*. Sold to Tidewater Commercial Company Incorporated of Monrovia, renamed *Titanus* in 1962 and broken up at Mihara in Japan in 1969.

Danae 1945 54 71.0x65.0x17.0 Steam Turbine — —
B W. Pickersgill & Son Limited, Sunderland.
Built as tug TID 155 and purchased by Alfred Holt & Company in 1947 for harbour operations at Hong Kong and renamed *Danae*. Sold to Sarawak Company (1959) Limited, Kuching, becoming *Hailey*.

Dardanus (4) 1920 9,503 485.6x62.3x35.8 Diesel 5,802 12½ knots
B Harland & Wolff, Glasgow.
Built for Glen Line as *Glenapp* for the Far East service. When built, she was the largest motorship in the world. However, they were underpowered, with a speed of 12 ½ knots, and in 1929, superchargers were fitted to *Glenapp* and her three sisters. She was transferred to the Ocean Steamship Company in

Tantalus (3).

Deucalion (4).

Dymas.

Pyrrhus (3).

1949, becoming *Dardanus* to operate on the Australian service. In 1956, she was laid up at Holy Loch and arrived at Inverkeithing on 19 July the following year to be broken up by Thos. W. Ward.

Deucalion (4) 1920 9,513 485.6x62.3x35.8 Diesel 5,859 12½ knots
B Harland & Wolff, Glasgow.
Dardanus class. Delivered to Glen Line as *Glenogle* and transferred to the Ocean Steamship Company in 1949 and renamed *Deucalion*. She was broken up at Briton Ferry in 1956.

Dolius (2) 1922 9,802 485.6x62.3x35.8 Diesel 5,938 12½ knots
B Harland & Wolff, Glasgow.
Dardanus class. Delivered to Glen Line as *Glengarry*, and in November 1922, she went aground in the Whangpo River. In 1925, she was in a collision with the tug *Heathercock* at Leith and was renamed *Glenstrae* in 1939. She was damaged in an air attack at the Royal Docks, London, in 1940 and transferred to the Ocean Steamship Company and renamed *Dolius* in 1949. She collided with the dock wall at Gladstone Dock, Liverpool, in July 1952 as she was sailing to Glasgow to discharge part of her cargo, causing serious damage to her starboard block casing. It was decided that it would not be economic to repair her and she was sent to Briton Ferry, where she arrived on 20 August to be demolished by Thos. W. Ward.

Dymas 1922 9,461 485.6x62.3x35.8 Diesel 5,789 12½ knots
B Harland & Wolff, Glasgow.
Dardanus class. Delivered to Glen Line as *Glenbeg* and transferred to the Ocean Steamship Company in 1949 as *Dymas*. She was broken up at Dalmuir by W. H. Arnott Young & Company in 1954.

Peleus (2) 1949 10,093 489.4x68.3x35.2 Steam Turbine 5,888 18½ knots
B Cammell, Laird & Company, Birkenhead.
Delivered to Ocean Steamship Company in 1949 and arrived at Kaohsiung on 18 February 1972 to be broken up.

Pyrrhus (3) 1949 10,093 489.4x68.3x35.2 Steam Turbine 5,898 18½ knots
B Cammell, Laird & Company, Birkenhead.
Sister to *Peleus*. On 12 November 1964, she caught fire in Huskisson Dock, Liverpool, and it took firefighters over twelve hours to control the blaze. The

Aegis Saga ex-*Ulysses* (5). (Victor Young)

Teiresias (2).

ship was abandoned twice during this operation, as there were fears for her stability in view of the amount of water pumped into her. She survived and was repaired and returned to service for a further eight years, as she arrived at Kaohsiung on 19 September 1972 to be broken up.

Patroclus (4)/ Philoctetes (2) 1950 10,109 489.4x68.3x35.2 Steam Turbine 5,923 18½ knots
B Vickers, Armstrong & Company, Newcastle, for the China Mutual Steam Navigation Company.
Sister to *Peleus*. On 28 November 1962, she went aground in Tokyo Bay. She caught fire at Glasgow in February 1967. Transferred to the Glen Line in 1972, becoming *Glenalmond*, and left Swansea as the *Philoctetes* on 21 November that year to be broken up by Chai Tai Steel Enterprises at Taiwan.

Perseus (3) 1950 10,109 489.4x68.3x35.2 Steam Turbine 5,923 18½ knots
B Vickers, Armstrong & Company, Newcastle, for the China Mutual Steam Navigation Company.
Sister to *Peleus*. She sailed on her maiden voyage on 21 April 1950. Arrived at Kaohsiung on 5 January 1973 to be broken up.

Ulysses (5) 1949 8,976 453.0x61.6x38.0 Steam Turbine 5,303 —
B Joseph L. Thompson & Sons, Sunderland, as the *Silverholly* for the Silver Line.
She was taken over by the China Mutual Steam Navigation Company, completed as *Ulysses*, and sailed on her maiden voyage from Birkenhead to the Far East in August 1949. The original passenger accommodation was allocated to the engineer officers and the passenger lounge became the officers' recreation room and pub. However, her air conditioning equipment could not cope with the heat of the tropics. She was sold to N. D. Papalios, Aegis Group, in 1971, becoming *Aegis Saga*, under the Greek flag, with Apsyrtos Shipping as her owners. She was scrapped in China in 1974.

Teiresias (2)/Telemachus (5) 1950 8,924 453.0x61.6x38.0 Steam Turbine 5,272 —
B Joseph L. Thompson & Sons, Sunderland, for the Silver Line.
Sister to *Ulysses*. She was launched as *Silverelm* and completed for NSM 'Oceaan' as *Teiresias*. In 1960, she was transferred to the British flag and renamed *Telemachus*, owned by the Ocean Steamship Company. In 1971, she was sold to the Aegis Group, N. D. Papalios, and renamed *Aegis Courage*, with Anax Shipping Company as owners. On 25 January 1973, she sailed from Yawata, Kyushu, in Japan to be broken up in China.

Teucer (4)/Telamon (3) 1950 8,922 453.0x61.6x38.0 Steam Turbine 5,273 —
B Joseph L. Thompson & Sons, Sunderland, for the Silver Line.
Sister to *Ulysses*. Launched as *Silverlaurel* and completed as *Teucer* for NSM 'Oceaan'. She was transferred to the British flag in 1960 as *Telamon*, owned by the China Mutual Steam Navigation Company. Sold in 1971 to the Aegis

group, N. D. Papalios, and renamed *Aegis Epic*, owned by the Apsyrtos Shipping Company and broken up in 1973.

Helenus (2) 1949 10,125 496.3x69.3x34.7 Steam Turbine 5,922 18½ knots
B Harland & Wolff, Belfast.
She was the first of a class of four vessels.
On 9 November 1949, as she was loading in Gladstone Dock, Liverpool, a fire broke out on shore. *Helenus* and *Dardanus* were loading at No. 2 branch; *Pyrrhus* and *Calchas* were discharging at No. 1 branch and were moved to safer berths. However, it was decided that *Helenus* and *Dardanus* should sail even though they were only partly loaded. She gave service on the Australian routes and arrived at Kaohsiung on 11 July 1972 to be broken up.

Jason (4) 1950 10,160 496.3x69.3x34.7 Steam Turbine 5,936 18½ knots
B Swan Hunter & Wigham Richardson, Newcastle.
Helenus class. She transported the Australian equestrian team from Sydney to Liverpool for the Olympic Games in Rome in 1960. Special facilities were constructed on the hatches, which were filled with sand to allow the horses to exercise. After twenty-two years service to the company, she arrived at Kaohsiung on 23 May 1972 to be broken up.

Hector (5) 1950 10,125 496.3x69.3x34.7 Steam Turbine 5,992 18½ knots
B Harland & Wolff, Belfast.
Helenus class. Built for the Australian service. Launched by Clement Atlee, the British Prime Minister, in July 1949 and sailed on her maiden voyage on 25 April the following year. She arrived at Kaohsiung on 5 July 1972 to be broken up.

Ixion (3) 1951 10,125 496.3x69.3x34.7 Steam Turbine 5,919 18½ knots
B Harland & Wolff, Belfast.
Helenus class. Completed for the Ocean Steamship Company's Australian service. She was sold to Salvamiento y Demolici SA to be broken up in Spain in 1972.

Nestor (4)/Orestes (5) 1952 7,802 464.9x64.3x31.1 Steam Turbine 4,368 —
B Caledon Shipbuilding & Engineering Company, Dundee.
When delivered, she was placed on the Australian services and transferred to the Glen Line in 1968, becoming *Glenaffric*, returning to the Blue Funnel Line two years later as *Orestes*. In 1971, she was sold to the Aegis Group, N. D. Papalios, and renamed *Aegis Dignity*, owned by Adelais Maritime Company of Cyprus and Kimon Cia Nav. SA of Piraeus. Sold in 1973 to be broken up in China.

Neleus (2) 1953 7,802 464.9x64.3x31.1 Steam Turbine 4,368 —
B Caledon Shipbuilding & Engineering Company, Dundee, for the China Mutual Steam Navigation Company.
Nestor class. Sailed on her maiden voyage on 21 March 1953 and was sold to Akamas Shipping Company, Cyprus, in 1971 becoming *Aegis Fable*, and *Aegis Trust* the following year, owned by Alicarnassos Shipping Company. She left Niigata in Japan on 17 March 1974 to be broken up in Shanghai.

Theseus (2) 1955 7,804 464.9x64.3x31.1 Steam Turbine 4,242 —
B Caledon Shipbuilding & Engineering Company, Dundee.
Sold to Aegis Group, N. D. Papalios, renamed *Aegis Myth*, owned by the Alkividis Shipping SA of Panama in 1971, and becoming *Aegis Care*, owned by Syracusae Maritime Company the following year. She left Singapore on 4 November 1973 to be broken up at Shanghai.

Demodocus (2) 1955 7,968 452.9x62.4x35.3 Diesel 4,558 15 knots
B Vickers, Armstrong & Company, Newcastle.
First of a class of three Mark A5 ships. Built for the Ocean Steamship Company and transferred to Glen Line in 1970, becoming *Glenroy*, and back to the Blue Funnel Line two years later as *Demodocus*. Sold to Nan Yang Shipping Company, Macao, in 1973 and renamed *Hungsia*, operated by Dawn Maritime Corporation, Panama. In 1979, she was renamed *Hong Oi 137*, Bureau of Maritime Transport Administration, China, and she was broken up in China in 1985.

Hungsia ex-*Demodocus* (2). (Victor Young)

Diomed (5).

Dolius (3).

Diomed (5) 1956 7,980 452.9x62.4x35.3 Diesel 4,267 15 knots
B Caledon Shipbuilding & Engineering Company, Dundee, for the China Mutual Steam Navigation Company.
Demodocus class. She was designed as a cadet training ship. In 1970, she was transferred to the Glen Line, becoming *Glenbeg*, and suffered a fire later that year which took five hours to extinguish. In 1972, she returned to the British flag under the China Mutual Steam Navigation Company as *Diomed*. Sold to Nan Yang Shipping Company, Macao, in 1973, becoming *Kaising* under the Somali flag, and operating by Golden City Maritime Corporation SA. She was broken up at Kaohsiung in 1983.

Dolius (3) 1956 7,960 452.9x62.4x35.3 Diesel 4,262 15 knots
B Harland & Wolff, Belfast.
Demodocus class. Delivered to the Ocean Steamship Company and transferred to the Glen Line in1970, becoming *Glenfruin*, and *Dolius* again two years later. Sold to Nan Yang Shipping Company, Macao, in 1972 and renamed *Hungmien*, also under the Somali flag. In 1977, she was sold to the Bureau of Maritime Transportation, China, becoming *Hong Qi 119*. She was renamed *Zhan Dou 51* in 1985 and was broken up.

Antenor (4)/Dymas (2) 1957 7,965 452.9x62.4x35.3 Diesel 4,276 15 knots
B Vickers, Armstrong & Company, Newcastle.
Demodocus class. Delivered to the Ocean Steamship Company as the first of a class of three Mark A6 ships and transferred to the Glen Line in 1970 as *Glenlochy*. She returned to Blue Funnel as *Dymas* in 1972 and was sold to Nan Yang Shipping Company the following year, becoming *Kaiyun*. Purchased by Highseas Navigation Corporation SA of Panama in 1976 and broken up in 1982.

Achilles (5)/Dardanus (5) 1957 7,969 452.9x62.4x35.3 Diesel 4,287 15 knots
Delivered to the Ocean Steamship Company and renamed *Dardanus* in 1972. Sold to Nan Yang Shipping Company in the following year, becoming *Kiago*, and managed by Highseas Navigation Corporation of Panama in 1977. She arrived at Calcutta on 5 June 1982 to be broken up.

Ajax (4)/Deucalion (5) 1958 7,969 452.9x62.4x35.3 Diesel 4,268 15 knots
B Vickers, Armstrong & Company, Newcastle for the China Mutual Steam Navigation Company.

Above left: Ajax (4).

Above right: Menestheus (4).

Right: Med Endeavour ex-*Machaon* (3). (Victor Young)

Demodocus class. Renamed *Deucalion* in 1972 and sold to Brilliance Steamship Company in 1973, becoming *Kailock*, owned by Nan Yang Shipping Company. Broken up at Kaohsiung in 1982.

Menelaus (4) 1957 8,538 455.4x65.4x36.1 Diesel 4,698 16½ knots
B Caledon Shipbuilding & Engineering Company, Dundee.
Built for the Ocean Steamship Company and transferred to Elder Dempster Lines in 1972. Renamed *Mano* for the British & Burmese Steam Navigation Company. She became *Oti* in 1977 and was sold to Thenamaris Maritime Incorporated of Greece, renamed *Elstar*, and operated by Leon Rivera Lines. She was scrapped in South Korea in 1979.

Menestheus (2) 1958 8,510 455.4x65.4x36.1 Diesel 4,873 16½ knots
B Caledon Shipbuilding & Engineering Company, Dundee.
Menelaus class. Built for the Ocean Steamship Company, transferred to Elder Dempster Lines in 1977 as *Onitsha*, and sold to Thenamaris Maritime Incorporated of Greece, becoming *Elisland*, operated by Palermo Shipping Company of Cyprus. She arrived at Kaohsiung on 19 March 1979 to be broken up.

Machaon (3) 1959 8,529 455.4x65.4x36.1 Diesel 4,650 16½ knots
B Caledon Shipbuilding & Engineering Company, Dundee.
Menelaus class. Handed over to the Ocean Steamship Company and transferred to NSM 'Oceaan' in 1975 and to Elder Dempster Lines two years later, becoming *Obuasi*. The following year, she was sold to Thenamaris Maritime Incorporated of Piraeus, renamed *Elsea*, and then to Tartan Shipping Limited of Monrovia, becoming *Med Endeavour*. She was broken up at Kaohsiung in 1979.

Annoula II ex-*Melampus* (2).

Europe II ex-*Maron* (3). (Victor Young)

Memnon (6)/Stentor (5) 1959 8,504 455.4x65.4x36.1 Diesel 4,873 16½ knots
B Vickers, Armstrong & Company, for the China Mutual Steam Navigation Company.
In 1975, she was renamed *Stentor* for the South-East Asia to Australia service and was transferred to Elder Dempster Lines two years later as *Owerri*. The following year she was sold to Thenamaris Maritime Incorporated of Piraeus, operated by Henlow Shipping Corporation, and renamed *Europe*. She was laid up at Stylis in 1982 and renamed *Primus* in 1987 for the voyage to Alang, where she was broken up the following year.

Melampus (2) 1960 8,509 455.4x65.4x36.1 Diesel 4,668 16½ knots
B Vickers, Armstrong & Company, Newcastle.
Menelaus class. On 6 June 1967, she was trapped in the Suez Canal during the Six-Day War between Israel and Egypt. Sold to the underwriters in 1971, who sold her to the Grecomar Shipping Agency Limited. On 20 May 1975, she was towed to Trieste, and following an overhaul, she was sold to the Korissianev Shipping Company SA, becoming *Annoula II*. Fourteen ships were trapped in the canal and only *Münsterland* and *Norwind* were able to leave under their own power. When the German vessels arrived at Hamburg, their owners, Hapag Lloyd, reported that they were in fairly good condition, although their hulls were badly caked with mussel growth, but there was very little corrosion damage. Most of the cargoes remained in remarkably good condition, apart from the perishable goods and tinned foods. *Annoula II* was broken up at Gadani Beach in 1983.

Maron (3)/Rhexenor (3) 1960 8,529 455.4x65.4x36.1 Diesel 4,649 16½ knots
B Caledon Shipbuilding & Engineering Company, Dundee.
Menelaus class. Renamed *Rhexenor* in 1975 for the Asia to Australia service, and in 1977, she was transferred to Elder Dempster Lines and renamed *Opobo*. Sold three years later to Thenamaris Maritime Incorporated at Piraeus, becoming *Elfortune*, operated by the Belton Shipping Corporation of Monrovia and renamed *Europe II*. Laid up at Piraeus in 1982 and arrived at Aliaga from Piraeus for breaking up in 1987.

Gunung Djati 1936 16,662 578.0x72.0x25.1 Steam Turbine 9,981 18 knots
B Blohm & Voss, Hamburg, as *Pretoria* for Deutsche Ost-Afrika Linie.
She sailed on her maiden voyage on 19 December 1936 from Hamburg and Southampton to South Africa, but grounded off Calshot on Christmas Eve, remaining there until Boxing Day. She became an accommodation ship for the German Navy at Hamburg from 1939 and became a hospital ship in 1945.

Gunung Djati.

Centaur (3).

At the end of hostilities, she was taken over by the British Government and operated on trooping duties as *Empire Doon*, managed by the Orient Line for the Ministry of War Transport. However, on her first voyage, she had to be turned around at Port Said and was laid up later that year with boiler problems. In 1949, she was reboilered and given an extensive overhaul by John I. Thornycroft at Southampton and renamed *Empire Orwell*. In 1958, she was chartered to the Pan-Islamic Steamship Company to be used as a pilgrim carrier between Karachi and Jeddah, and following this work, she was laid up in the Kyles of Bute. In November that year, she was sold to Alfred Holt for the pilgim service and was renamed *Gunung Djati*, owned by the Ocean Steamship Company. Refitted at Barclay Curle & Company, on the Clyde, with accommodation for 106 first class passengers and 2,000 pilgrims. She sailed from Liverpool to Djakarta on 7 March 1959 to join *Tyndareus*. After completing three seasons, she was sold to the Indonesian Government and to P. T. Maskapai Pelajaran 'Sang Saka' of Djakarta in 1965. The Pan-Islamic Steamship Company took her over in 1968, and she was converted to diesel engines at Hong Kong in 1973. She was given a major refit at Hong Kong two years later, and in 1980, she was returned to the Indonesian Government, becoming a transport ship and naval accommodation vessel at Tanjung Priok, renamed *Kri Tanjung Pandan*, pendant number 971. She was sold to be broken up at Kaohsiung in 1987.

Centaur (3) 1964 8,262 480.9x66.3x38.9 Diesel 4,409 20 knots
B John Brown & Company Limited, Glasgow.
Launched on 20 June 1963 by Mrs D. Bland, wife of the Prime Minister of Western Australia and completed at a cost of £2.5 million. She left Liverpool on her maiden voyage to Sydney on 20 January 1964 and operated on a three-weekly service from Fremantle and Western Australian ports to Singapore with accommodation for 190 first class passengers, refrigerated cargo, 4,500 sheep and 700 cattle. She took her first sailing on charter to the Australian Chambers of Trade mission. Transferred to the China Mutual Steam Navigation Company in 1967 and, in 1973, to the ownership of Eastern Fleets Limited section, managed by the Straits Steamship Company Limited of Singapore. In 1978, she was owned by Blue Funnel (SEA) Pte Limited of Singapore and took her final sailing from Fremantle on 15 September 1981. The following year, she was chartered to the St Helena Shipping Company to replace their ship which had been chartered for Falkland Islands service. She arrived at Avonmouth on 29 November 1982, and it was hoped that she would find a new home on the St Helena service. However, she was in poor condition and suffered machinery problems and sailed from Avonmouth to Singapore via Cape Town and Fremantle on 18 October 1983. Her funnel was repainted in Blue Funnel colours at Cape Town, and she was laid up when she

Priam (5).

Peisander (2).

arrived at Singapore. In 1985, she was sold to Shanghai Hai Xing Shipping Company and became *Hai Long* and *Hai Da* the following year. She survived until 1995, when she was scrapped at Xinhui, Guangdong, China.

Priam (5) 1966 12,094 563.8x77.9x44.0 Diesel 6,471 21 knots
B Vickers, Armstrong & Company, Newcastle.
The first ship in a class of eight, for the Ocean Steamship Company and the Glen Line. She was one of four ships of the class sold to C. Y. Tung in 1978 for conversion to cellular container vessels. *Priam* was renamed *Oriental Champion* and was transferred to Carterfold Shipping Company in 1980, sold to Vanderhoff Shipping Company, Panama, in 1982, and to Island Investment & Agency Corporation Limited and Wattling Navigation Incorporated, Panama, two years later. On 18 October 1985, she was hit by an Iraqi missile in the Persian Gulf, and she was towed to Bahrain, where it was decided that it was not economic to repair her, and she left in tow on 11 December to be broken up at Kaohsiung.

Patroclus (5) 1966 12,094 563.8x77.9x44.0 Diesel 6,471 21 knots
B Mitsubishi Heavy Industries, Nagasaki, Japan.
Phrontis class. Delivered to Glen Line as *Glenalmond* and was actually the first of the *Priam* class to enter service. Transferred to the China Mutual Steam Navigation Company in 1973, becoming *Patroclus*, and was employed in a joint service with the Swedish East Asiatic Company and operated in their colours. In 1974, she was transferred to NSM 'Oceaan' and returned to British registry four years later, when she was laid up prior to operating on a joint Ben-Ocean service. Sold to Rajab & Company of Jeddah in 1982, becoming *Rajab 1*. On 18 July 1984, on a voyage from Bangkok to Dubai, she arrived at Port Rashid on fire. It took four days to extinguish the fire, but she was severely damaged, and on 20 August, her main engine was damaged by salt water. Consequently, she was sold to Molasses Trading & Export Company, renamed *Sahar*, and arrived at Gadani Beach on 26 November to be broken up.

Peisander (2) 1967 12,094 563.1x77.9x44.0 Diesel 6,471 21 knots
B Vickers, Armstrong & Company, Newcastle.
Priam class. Delivered to the Ocean Steamship Company and transferred to the China Mutual Navigation Company in 1972 and was laid up at Falmouth in 1978 and sold to C. Y. Tung, becoming *Oriental Exporter*. Renamed *Main Express* in 1981 on charter to Hapag and sold to Island Investment & Agency Corporation and Wattling Navigation Incorporated, Liberia, in 1984, and renamed *Oriental Exporter*. She arrived at Kaohsiung to be broken up on 10 September 1986.

Protesilaus (2) 1967 12,094 563.1x77.9x44.0 Diesel 6,471 21 knots
B Vickers, Armstrong & Company, Newcastle, for the China Mutual Steam Navigation Company.

Oriental Importer ex-*Protesilaus* (2). (Victor Young)

Priam class. Sold in 1978 to Balcombe Company Limited, Hong Kong, renamed *Oriental Importer*, and to Carbrook Shipping Limited in 1979, when she was converted to a cellular container vessel. Two years later, she was placed on charter to Hapag and renamed *Main Express*. She was transferred to Flint Shipping Limited, Panama, in 1982, becoming *Oriental Importer*, and to Island Investment & Agency Corporation Limited and Wattling Navigation Incorporated, Panama, in 1984. On 1 June 1985, she was hit by two rockets on a voyage from Damman to Kuwait and was scrapped at Kaohsiung later that year.

Prometheus (4) 1967 12,094 563.1x77.9x44.0 Diesel 6,471 21 knots
B Vickers, Armstrong & Company, Newcastle.
Completed for the Ocean Steamship Company and transferred to the China Mutual Navigation Company in 1972. Sold to Blound Company Limited of Hong Kong, renamed *Oriental Merchant*, and converted to a cellular container ship in 1979. Renamed *Oriental Merchant 1* and then *Oriental Merchant* in 1980 and sold to Island Investment & Agency Corporation Limited and Wattling Navigation Incorporated, Panama, in 1984. She arrived at Kaohsiung on 21 March 1985 to be broken up.

Phrontis (2) 1967 12,299 563.8x77.9x44.0 Diesel 6,573 21 knots
B Mitsubishi H.I., Nagasaki.
Priam class. Completed as *Pembrokeshire* for Glen Line and transferred to the Ocean Steamship Company and the China Mutual Steam Navigation Company in 1972, becoming *Phrontis*. She was chartered to Wilhelm Wilhelmsen in 1978 and sold to Gulf Shipping Lines, London, in 1982, becoming *Gulf Osprey*. The following year, she was sold to the Islamic Republic of Iran Shipping Lines and renamed *Iran Ejtehad*. Sold to be broken up at Gadani Beach in 1995 arriving there as *Dolphin VIII*.

Phemius (5) 1967 12,094 563.8x77.9x44.0 Diesel 6,471 21 knots
B John Brown & Company, Glasgow.
Priam class. Completed as *Glenfinlas* for Glen Line, transferred to Blue Funnel Line in 1972 as *Phemius* and sold to the China Navigation Company in 1978 and renamed *Kweichow*. She was sold to the Saudi Venture Corporation of Jeddah, becoming *Saudi Kawther* in 1983 and was broken up in China the following year.

Top: Phemius (5).

Above: Saudi Kawther ex-*Phemius* (5). (Victor Young)

Perseus (4) 1967 12,094 563.8x77.9x44.0 Diesel 6,471 21 knots
B Vickers, Armstrong & Company, Newcastle.
Priam class. Completed for the Glen Line as *Radnorshire* and transferred to the China Mutual Steam Navigation Company in 1973, becoming *Perseus*. Sold to the China Navigation Company in 1978, renamed Kwangsi and sold again in 1981, becoming *Asia Dragon*. The following year, she was sold to the Saudi Venture Corporation of Jeddah and renamed *Saudi ZamZam*. She was hit by shells in Shatt-el-Arab during the Iran/Iraq War in 1984 and was broken up in China later that year.

Sarpedon (6) 1939 7,151 507.0x66.0x38.0 Diesel 3,455 17 knots
B Nederlandsche Scheep, Maats., Amsterdam.
She was ordered by the Glen Line and was delivered to them as *Denbighshire*. She sailed in convoys to Malta and was attacked and damaged while berthed at Valletta, and in 1945, she operated in the Pacific and was transferred to the China Mutual Steam Navigation Company in 1967, becoming *Sarpedon*. She arrived at Kaohsiung on 11 August 1969 to be broken up.

Dardanus (6) 1939 9,311 507.0x66.0x38.0 Diesel 4,811 17 knots
B Burmeister & Wain, Copenhagen.
Sister to *Sarpedon*. Ordered by the Glen Line and launched as *Glengarry*. In May 1940, she was captured by the Germans, who had seized the port of Copenhagen, and renamed *Meersburg*, managed by the Hamburg Amerika Line. She later became a depot ship, servicing submarine flotillas 25 and 27, based at Kiel, and was converted into a mine-laying Armed Merchant Cruiser as *Hansa*, fitted with nine 3-inch guns, twenty-six anti-aircraft guns and four torpedo tubes. However, she was never used for this purpose, and at the end of the war, she was taken over by British authorities in May 1945 and renamed *Empire Humber*. Two years later, she became a member of the Glen Line fleet as *Glengarry*, was transferred to Blue Funnel, becoming *Dardanus* in 1970. and renamed *Glengarry* again for her voyage to the breakers at Sakaide, Japan, the following year.

Titan (4) 1972 113,551 1090.3x149.9x67.9 Steam Turbine 90,609 15½ knots
B A/B Gotaverken, Gothenburg.
Delivered to Ocean Titan Limited and transferred to Elder Dempster in 1973. She was sold to Mobil Shipping & Transportation Company of Monrovia in 1975 and renamed *Mobil Condor*. Laid up in Greece because of the reduction in demand for oil at the time, she was sold to Nissho Iwai Corporation to be broken up at Pusan in Korea in 1982.

Top: Titan (4).

Above: Tantalus (5). (Victor Young)

Tantalus (5) 1972 120,787 1074.7x164.2x62.9 Steam Turbine 98,631 15½ knots
B Nippon Kokan at Tsu for the China Mutual Steam Navigation Company as an ore/oil carrier.
In July 1978, she was laid up for several months, and again in 1982, this time at the Ocean Dock at Southampton for two years. Sold to the Norwegian Bulk Shipping, becoming *Tantra*, owned by Orca Shipping Company of Cyprus. Two years later, she was purchased by Yellow Diamond Company and renamed *Antarctica*. On 25 November 1986, she was attacked by Iraqi aircraft at Larak Island in the Persian Gulf and was seriously damaged by fire and was towed to China to be broken up.

Achilles (6). (Victor Young)

Sideris ex-*Antenor* (5). (Victor Young)

Achilles (6) 1972 16,406 579.9x75.2x35.0 Diesel 10,420 15 knots
B Mitsui Shipbuilding & Engineering Company, Fijingata, Japan.
She was completed for the Blue Funnel Line, with the Ocean Steamship Company as managers and transferred to Elder Dempster ownership in 1974 and to Blue Funnel Bulkships Limited three years later. In 1979, she was sold to Silverdale Shipping Company, Bermuda, and managed by Flores Maritime Pte, Singapore, in 1983. Renamed *Arko* and sold to Transocean MA of St Vincent in 1987, renamed *Patmos*, owned by Stathatos of Greece in 1988, and *Winner*, owned by Sunflower Shipping Company in 1995. She arrived at Alang to be broken up on 15 April 1998.

Agamemnon (4) 1972 16,402 579.9x75.2x35.0 Diesel 10,422 15 knots
B Mitsui Shipbuilding & Engineering Company, Fujingata, Japan.
Achilles class. Delivered to Ocean Fleets Limited and managed by Elder Dempster Lines, transferred to Elder Dempster ownership in 1974 and to Blue Funnel Bulkship Limited three years later. In 1978, she was sold to Protoporos Maritime Corporation, becoming *Protoporos*. Placido Shipping Corporation, renamed *Alicia* in 1984, and to the Black Sea Shipping Company, Odessa, the following year, becoming *Anapa*. In 1991, she was purchased by Canopus Shipping SA of Greece, becoming *North Star*, and to Aldebaran Shipping, Panama, in 1993 and renamed *Freedom K*. She arrived at Alang on 27 September 2000 to be broken up.

Antenor (5) 1972 16,406 579.9x75.2x34.5 Diesel 10,420 15 knots
B Mitsui Shipbuilding & Engineering Company, Fujinata, Japan.
Achilles class. Handed over to Ocean Fleets Limited, transferred to Elder Dempster in 1974 and to Blue Funnel Bulkships Limited in 1977. She was sold to Mermaid Sea Carriers Corporation of Liberia in 1978, becoming *Sideris*, Joh. Solstad, Skudeneshavn, in 1989, renamed *Solbuk*, and Seacross Navigation Company of Panama in 1996 as *Kyklades K*. She arrived at Chittagong on 22 May 2001 to be broken up.

Anchises (5) 1973 16,406 579.9x75.2x35.0 — 10,420 15 knots
B Mitsui Shipbuilding & Engineering Company, Fujingata, Japan.
Achilles class. Delivered to Ocean Fleets Limited, transferred to Blue Funnel Bulkships Limited in 1977, and sold to the Black Sea Shipping Company in 1984, renamed *Aytodar*. Sold to a Malta company in 1991, becoming *Aitodor*, and arrived at Alang on 14 January 1997 to be broken up.

Ajax (5) 1973 16,406 579.9x75.2x35.0 Diesel 10,420 15 knots
B Mitsui Shipbuilding & Engineering Company, Fujingata, Japan.
Achilles class. Delivered to Ocean Titan Limited, transferred to Blue Funnel Bulkships Limited in 1977 and sold to Black Sea Shipping Company in 1984, becoming *Adler*. Sold to Neptune Maritime Company of Panama in 1992, renamed *North Wind*, and to A. E. Nomikos of Greece the following year,

Above left: Anchises (5). (Victor Young)

Above right: Ajax (5). (Victor Young)

Left: Troilus (5).

becoming *Cannes*. She was sold to United States owners in 1999 and renamed *Elizabeth*.

Troilus (5) 1974 127,265 1087.7x183.9x66.4 Steam Turbine 107,013 15½ knots
B Mitsui Shipbuilding & Engineering Company, Chiba.
Delivered to Ocean Troilus Limited and sold to Al-Dhafrah Tanker Company of Monrovia in 1975, becoming *Al-Dhafrah*. After a brief career of only eleven years, she was sold to Smit Tak International Ocean Towage & Salvage, renamed *Alda*, and was scrapped at Kaohsiung in 1985.

Helenus (3) 1973 30,078 718.0x55.9x39.7 Diesel 22,422 15 knots
B Burmeister & Wain, Copenhagen, as a bulk carrier built for Rea Limited and managed by Ocean Titan Limited.
Owned by Ocean Helenus Limited in 1977 and converted into a car carrier in 1978. Sold to Eurocolor Shipping Limited of Cyprus in 1983 and renamed *Seafarer*. She was converted back to a bulk carrier in 1988 and sold to Sommersby Shipping Limited (Thenamaris), Valletta, in 1997 and renamed *Seafarer 1*. On 21 May 1998, she collided with *Fedra* and was repaired at Cadiz and was broken up at Alang in 2000.

Helenus (3).

Laertes (5).

Hector (6) 1973 30,078 718.0x55.9x39.7 Diesel 22,422 15 knots
B Burmeister & Wain, Copenhagen.
Helenus class. Delivered to Cory Maritime Services and sold to Cast Motorvessels Limited in 1979 and renamed *Cast Orca*. In 1982, she was bought by Ocean Tramping Company of Hong Kong, becoming *Tramco Asia*, and by Armadora Maribella SA of Greece the following year and renamed *Marijeannie*. She arrived at Alang on 1 April 1998 to be broken up.

Cyclops (4) 1975 32,576 690.7x53.4x40.8 Diesel 22,605 16½ knots
B Van der Giessen-de-Noord BV, Krimpen, as a products carrier.
Delivered to Ocean Titan Limited and transferred to Blue Funnel Bulkships Limited in 1977. She was the largest vessel to have been laid up on the River Fal when she was there in 1982. She was moved to Falmouth the following May and was sold to Pequat Shipping Corporation of Greece and renamed *Procyon*. She became *Nova Europe* when owned by Rethymnis & Kulukundis of London in 1990. She was sold to Barcuera Cia Nav. SA of Panama, renamed *Demos* in 1995, and was broken up in India in 2002.

Charon (3) 1975 24,512 636.8x99.9x49.5 Diesel 14,865 14½ knots
B Sasebo Heavy Industries, Sasebo, Japan.
Delivered to Koninklijke NSM 'Oceaan' and transferred to Blue Funnel Line Limited in 1978. She was sold to Ceres Hellenic Shipping Enterprises in 1985, renamed *Finesse L*, later *Finesse*, and sold to Yellow Star Shipping Limited of Oslo, becoming *Yellow Star* in 1995.

Clytoneus (3) 1976 32,576 690.7x53.4x40.8 Diesel 22,605 16½ knots
B Van der Giessen-de-Noord B.V., Krimpen.
Delivered to Ocean Titan Limited, transferred to Blue Funnel Bulkships Limited in 1977, and sold to Transpetrol Nav. Pte Limited of Singapore in 1985 and renamed *Affinity*. Purchased by Transporti Internazionali Petroliferi of Italy in 1987, renamed *Cervino*, and Impresa Transporti Marittimi of Italy in 1989, becoming *Nunki*. She was broken up at Alang in 2000.

Laertes (5) 1976 11,804 533.1x74.1x43.9 Diesel 6,285 18 knots
B Kherson Shipyard, Kherson, USSR, for the China Mutual Steam Navigation Company.
She was a vessel of the Dnepr class and registered in Amsterdam and designed to carry 404 containers as well as having 19,570 cubic metres for break bulk cargo. *Laertes* and *Lycaon* were two-decked with five hatches forward of the engine-room and superstructure, and twin-operated hatch openings were provided for the four main holds. Cargo was handled by seven 12-tonne cranes and a heavy swinging derrick capable of 63 tonnes. Propelled by a six-cylinder Burmeister & Wain engine, giving a service speed of 18.2 knots. It was originally planned to operate the two sisters under the Dutch flag, but

Eleftheria K ex-*Lycaon* (3). (Victor Young)

Menelaus (5). (Victor Young)

when they both arrived at Birkenhead on 6 January 1977, they were registered at Amsterdam but were flying the Red Ensign. However, this was quickly changed to Liverpool by staff at the Odyssey Works at Birkenhead. She operated on the Japan to Persian Gulf service, was transferred to Elder Dempster Lines in 1982 and requisitioned by the British Government for service in the Falkland Islands that year. Sold to Dimskal Shipping of Panama in 1983, renamed *Evia Luck*, and then to Sponge Maritime Company, Cyprus, in 1987 and renamed *Vigor*. In 1992, she became *Joy D*, owned by Signet Shipping Company of Cyprus, and arrived at Alang on 26 June 1998 to be broken up.

Lycaon (3) 1976 11,804 533.1x74.1x43.9 Diesel 6,285 18 knots
B Kherson Shipyard, Kherson, USSR, for the China Mutual Steam Navigation Company.
Laertes class. She arrived at Birkenhead on 6 January 1977, on the same tide as her sister *Laertes*. Chartered to work in the Caribbean and South America in 1979 and laid up at Falmouth in 1983, when she was requisitioned by the British Government for Falkland Islands service and a helipad was fitted. The following year, she was laid up on the Tyne at Newcastle Quay, transferred to Blue Funnel Bulkships Limited in 1985 and sold to Mersey Transport Incorporated, Panama, and renamed *Chrysovalandou Faith*. She was also purchased by Estuary Shipping of Panama that year, becoming *Eleftheria K*. She arrived at Alang on 13 April 1998 to be broken up.

Nestor (5) 1977 78,951 275.0x27.4x12.3 Steam Turbine 51,244 19½ knots
B Chantiers de l'Atlantique, as an LNG carrier.
As there was no immediate work for her, she went straight into lay-up at Loch Striven. She had been designed and built for a proposed service between Indonesia and California and she remained at Loch Striven until she was sold to Bonny Gas Transport Limited and renamed *LNG Port Harcourt*. She was towed to Inverkip in April 1992 and entered dry dock at Brest and then laid up there. On 7 January 1994, she finally sailed from Brest to Lumut, and when she arrived there, she was laid up in Brunei Bay. She was then sent to Singapore for refit and loaded her first cargo of LNG at Lumut in December that year. In 1999, she transferred to the company's service in Europe. She cost Alfred Holt's £62.4 million and never carried a commercial cargo for them.

Menelaus (5) 1977 16,031 540.0x46.6x34.8 Diesel 8,666 18 knots
B Mitsubishi Heavy Industries, Nagasaki.
Menelaus and three other vessels were on charter to the Ocean Steamship Company from Airlease Holdings International Nominees (Moorgate) Limited, a subsidiary of British Petroleum. BP had decided that, rather than cancel an order for two super tankers and suffer significant penalty charges, they would have these four vessels built and leased out on charter. *Menelaus* was renamed *Barber Menelaus* for the Barber Blue Sea service in December, 1980, *Menelaus* in 1984, and transferred to Elder Dempster Lines the following year. In 1989, she was sold to Worlder

Barber Memnon ex-*Memnon* (7). (Victor Young)

Melampus (3). (Victor Young)

Shipping Limited of Hong Kong, becoming *Trade Green*, and to Georgian Maritime Corporation, St Vincent, in 1995 and renamed *North Sea*, and on charter to Mediterranean Shipping Company, *MSC Nicole*. She became *North Sea* again in 1997 and was laid up at Eleusis Bay in Greece in 1998, arriving at Alang on 14 January 2002 to be broken up.

Memnon (7) 1977 16,031 540.0x46.6x34.8 Diesel 8,666 18 knots
B Mitsubishi Heavy Industries, Nagasaki, Japan.
Menelaus class. Owned by Airlease International Nominees. She was renamed *Barber Memnon* in 1980 to operate for Barber Blue Sea, managed by Elder Dempster Lines, and *Memnon* in 1984. Chartered to Lloyd Brasileiro later that year, she became *Lloyd San Francisco*. Sold in 1989 to Pacific International Lines Pte, Singapore, she was renamed *Hai Xiong*, and arrived at Mumbai on 31 December 2001 to be broken up.

Melampus (3) 1977 16,031 540.0x46.6x34.8 Diesel 8,666 18 knots
B Mitsubishi Heavy Industries, Nagasaki, Japan.
Menelaus class. Owned by Airlease International Nominees. She was chartered to Barber Blue Sea in 1980, managed by Elder Dempster Lines and chartered to the NYK Line in 1988. Sold to CMB the following year, becoming *CMB Ebony*, transferred to Bocimar NV in 1997, renamed *Ebony* in 2000, *Delmas Bandia* in 2001 and *Ebony* again in 2002. She arrived at Alang to be broken up on 3 October 2002 and was beached the following week.

Menestheus (3) 1977 16,031 540.0x46.6x34.8 Diesel 8,666 18 knots
B Mitsubishi Heavy Industries, Nagasaki, Japan.
Menelaus class. Owned by Airlease International Nominees and delivered to Ocean Fleets Limited. Chartered to Barber Blue Sea in 1980, and renamed *Barber Menetheus* and *Menetheus* again in 1983. She was chartered in 1984 to Woermann Lines and then to Lloyd Brasileiro and renamed *Lloyd Parana*. Reverted to West African service for Ocean Fleets in 1986, becoming *Apapa Palm*, and chartered to CAVN in 1988. She was sold to CMB in 1989 and renamed *CMB Esprit* and chartered to Woermann Lines as *Woermann Expert*. She operated for Bocimar NV in 1997 and was owned by Twinsea Shipping Company in 2002 as *Expert* and *Delmas Sycamore* for on charter to Delmas in 2001. *Expert*, *Clipper Itajai II* and *King Spirit* in 2007.

Plumleaf 1960 12,549 560.0x72.1x39.1 Diesel 7,418 15 knots
B Blyth Shipbuilding & Dry Dock Company Limited, Blyth.
She was built for William Cory & Son as Corheath and chartered by the Admiralty while on the stocks and completed as a Fleet Replenishment vessel. She was brought into the ownership of Blue Funnel Bulkships in 1977 but continued a Royal Naval Fleet Auxiliary vessel. On 17 December 1986, she arrived at Kaohsiung to be broken up.

Maron (4) 1980 16,482 164.5x26.0x14.2 metres Diesel 8,872 18 knots
B Scott's Shipbuilding & Engineering Co. Limited, Greenock.

Maron (4).

Myrmidon (5).

Launched by Lady Belinda Morse, wife of the chairman of Lloyds Bank. She sailed on her maiden voyage from Middlesbrough to West Africa for the Elder Dempster Lines, becoming *Studland Bay* on charter to P&O in 1981 and back to *Maron* two years later. In 1986, she was sold to Al-Mubarak Shipping & Trading Company and to Omega Limited of Bermuda, becoming *Baltic Adventurer* and *Rainbow Avenue*. Two years later, she was sold to Cenargo Limited of London and renamed *Merchant Patriot*. She was renamed *CMB Enterprise* in 1989, *Woermann Ubangi* in 1990, *Merchant Patriot* in 1991, *Lanka Amitha* in 1992, and *Merchant Patriot* again in 1994. On 30 December 1997, she was in danger of sinking in position 28.30N 75.48W as a ruptured seawater pipe had flooded the engine-room and heavy seas were making progress impossible. The crew of twenty-eight were taken off by the US Coastguard and the ship was towed to Freeport, where she arrived on 5 January 1998. She was sold to Demeresa of Mexico for breaking up, which commenced on 25 June that year.

Mentor (3) 1980 16,482 164.5x26.0x14.2 metres Diesel 8,872 18 knots
B Scott's Shipbuilding & Engineering Company, Greenock.
Maron class. Launched by Lady Alexander, wife of Sir Lindsay Alexander, chairman of the Ocean Group. Delivered to Elder Dempster Lines and chartered to Overseas Container Line in 1981 and renamed *City of London*. She was laid up on the River Fal in 1982 as *Mentor*, returning to the Overseas Container Lines service in 1984. Sold to Hake Shipping Company Limited of Cyprus in 1985, becoming *Normannia*. Renamed *Als Reliance* in 1986, *Hoegh Normania* in 1988, *Rickmers Hangzhou* in 1989, *St Nikolas 1* in 1990, *DSR-Shanghai*, *Palmas* and *DG Endeavour* in 1994, and *Tamatiki* in 1995, when she was sold to Tamahine Shipping Limited. She arrived at Alang on 7 May 2001 to be broken up.

Myrmidon (5) 1980 16,482 164.5x26.0x14.2 metres Diesel 8,872 18 knots
B Scott's Shipbuilding & Engineering Company, Greenock.
Maron class. Delivered to Elder Dempster Lines and chartered to GCM for a voyage to the Caribbean in 1981. She was chartered to the Ministry of Defence in 1982 during the Falklands Conflict, and in 1984, she was renamed *Cape Town Carrier* when chartered to Maritime Associated Carriers. Became *Myrmidon* again in 1985 and sold to the Nigerian Green Lines the following year, becoming *Bello Folawiyo*. In 1989, she was purchased by Cenargo Limited and renamed *CMB Exporter*, *Merchant Promise* in 1990, *Lanka Amila* in 1992, and *Merchant Promise* in 1993. She was sold to Tamapatcharee Shipping Limited of Hong Kong, becoming *Tamamonta* in 1994, and arrived at Alang on 16 January 2002 to be broken up.

Barber Perseus. (Victor Young)

Barber Priam 1979 21,747 749.6x105.8x66.3 Diesel 11,999 20½ knots
B Mitsubishi Heavy Industries, Nagasaki, Japan.
Delivered to Ocean Transport & Trading as a cargo and refrigerated vessel fitted with a stern ramp for roll-on/roll-off cargoes. In 1984, she was owned by Odysseus Shipping International Corporation of Panama and the Ocean Transport & Trading two years later. She was sold to the United States Military Sea Lift Command in 1986 for $25 million and renamed *Cape Henry* at Hampton Roads.

Barber Perseus 1979 21,747 749.6x105.8x66.3 Diesel 11,999 20½ knots
B Mitsubishi Heavy Industries, Nagasaki, Japan.
Sister of *Barber Priam*. Delivered to Speakshaw Limited, with Ocean Fleets as managers, later owned by Barber Menelaus Shipping Corporation, Panama, and by Perseus Shipping Limited of Panama in 1985. She was sold to Sweden Liners KB of Gothenburg and placed on charter to Rederi A/B Transatlantic and Wilhelmsen Lines, becoming *Talabot*. When she was handed over in Hong Kong, she was the last Blue Funnel vessel in service. She was sold to Wilhelmsen Lines in 1993 and was broken up in 2009.

Barber Hector 1984 49,326 859.6x105.8x68.9 Diesel 16,760 20 knots
B Hyundai Heavy Industries, South Korea.
She was built for the North America to the Far East and Persian Gulf service to carry heavy loads with a capacity for 630 cars and 2,464 containers. Trailers, wheeled cargo and heavy unit loads were loaded over a MacGregor Navire stern ramp capable of accepting 420-ton spread-out loads and wide enough to enable two-way loading and unloading to take place. Internal ramps allowed cargo to be transferred within the vessel to the various cargo decks. The cars were loaded over a portable car ramp through a door in the starboard side of the hull. The

containers were normally stored on the weather deck, although 200 refrigerated containers could be stowed on No. 3 and No. 4 deck. She was self-sustaining, carrying seven forklift trucks ranging from 4-tonne to 35-tonne capacity, complete with the various attachments, and four trailers, two of 60-tonne and two of 30-tonne capacity. A 40-tonne capacity deck crane was also provided. She was fitted with 2,300-hp bow and stern thrusters and accommodation for twenty-two crew, in separate cabins, with bathroom facilities. In 1988, she was sold to Swedish Liners KB of Gothenburg and chartered to Rederi A/B Transatlantic and to Wilhelmsen Lines of Norway and renamed *Taiko*. She was bought by Wilhelmsen Lines for $37 million in 1993, and in 2002, she was converted to a car carrier by Nantong Ocean Engineering, China.

Other Vessels

Argo 1875 580 208.0x26.3x16.0 — — 11 knots
B Scott & Company, Greenock.
She was Alfred Holt's private yacht and was also used as a cadet training ship. Sold in 1881.

Ranee 1881 617 185.0x27.1x13.6 — 378 9 knots
B Ramage & Ferguson, Leith.
Built for the Sarawak & Singapore Steamship Company and purchased by the East India Ocean Steamship Company in 1892; on charter to Alfred Holt since 1888. Renamed *Labuan* when transferred to Norddeutscher Lloyd in 1899, *Bin Seng* and *Pin Seng* when bought by Quah Seh Quan the following year. Transferred to the Eastern Shipping Company, Penang, in 1907 and sold to China in 1921. She was broken up in 1923.

Kongsee 1878 1,072 248.0x31.2x17.9 — 696 10 knots
B C. Mitchell & Company, Newcastle.
Built for the Netherlands Indies Steam Navigation Company and bought by T. C. Bogaardt, Singapore, in 1890, operating on Blue Funnel Line services and NSM 'Oceaan' in 1893. Purchased by Tan Kim Tinn in 1898, Philippine owners in 1899, renamed *Liscum* in 1901, and sold to Tuason & Sampedro at Manila in 1922, becoming Nuestra Senora de Alba. In 1934, she was purchased by Yung Shun Steamship Company of China, renamed *Yung Shun,* and was broken up in 1936.

Banjermassin 1886 428 174.0x23.7x12.2 — 261 9 knots
B Wigham Richardson & Company, Newcastle.
Built for Kho Soen Tjio Ang Eng, Banjermassin, and operated for Blue Funnel on services to Singapore. Owned by Alfred Holt's in 1889 and transferred to NSM 'Oceaan' in 1892 and the East India Ocean Steamship Company in 1896. Purchased by Norddeutscher Lloyd and renamed *Sulu* in 1899, becoming *Tan Auco* in 1900 when she was sold to Philippine owners. On 3 March 1901, she was abandoned on *Patras Sandbank* in the Philippines.

Devonhurst 1874 1,559 280.0x33.3x24.6 — 1,235 10 knots
B C. Mitchell & Company, Newcastle.
Built for H. Katz of Singapore for the Singapore to Calcutta and Nizagapatnam route. Sold to Netherlands India Steam Navigation Company in 1878 and owned by Atjeh Steamship Company of London in 1882 and bought by T. C. Bogaardt in 1888, operating on Blue Funnel services. On 8 March 1891, she was in a collision with *Strathendrick*, which later sank. Owned by Alfred Holt in 1892, and she was transferred to the East India Ocean Steamship Company in 1893 and was renamed *Kubo Maru* in 1896, when she was sold to Japanese interests and was wrecked on Kyushu the following year.

Normanby 1874 976 220.4x27.8x14.9 — 664 10 knots
B Henderson Coulborn, Renfrew.
Built for the Eastern & Australian Steamship Company and sold to J. S. Neave of Singapore in 1880. Purchased by Ong Kew Ho in 1884 and T. C. Bogaardt in 1891. Transferred to Alfred Holt ownership that year and to NSM 'Oceaan' in 1892. On a voyage from Manila to Singapore, she was wrecked near Pulu Bintang on 5 December 1893.

Maha Vajirunis 1881 1,176 253.0x32.2x17.5 — 704 10 knots
B C. Mitchell & Company, Newcastle.
Built for Atjeh Steamship Company of London and chartered to T. C. Bogaardt for service between Padang and Penang to Singapore in 1891, owned by Alfred Holt. Transferred to NSM 'Oceaan' in 1893 and was taken over by Koninklijke Paketvaart Maats the following year. She was broken up in 1907.

Charon 1896 1,920 278.0x41.1x20.8 — 1,237 9½ knots
B Workman, Clark & Company, Belfast.
Built for the East Ocean Steamship Company and transferred to Norddeutscher Lloyd in 1899, becoming *Bangkok*. Owned by Awakoku Kiodo KK Tokushma, Japan, in 1911 and renamed *Kiodo Maru* No. 13. Sold to Uchida Kisen KK in 1918, and renamed *Kyodo Maru* No. 13 in 1922 when owned by Ogina Kaisyo KK. Purchased by Oginuno Kaisho KK in 1933 and sunk in 1945.

Sinkiang 1954 6,057 471.8x61.7x40.7 — 3,207 17 knots
B Nederlandsche Dok & Sch Mij., Amsterdam.
Built for Wilhelm Wilhelmsen of Oslo as *Troubadour* and sold to the China Navigation Company in 1971, renamed *Sinkiang*. In 1973, she was owned by Eggar, Forrester (Holdings) Limited of London, and Blue Funnel Line, China Mutual Steam Navigation Company in 1976. The following year, she was owned by Taikoo Navigation Company, Hong Kong, with John Swire & Sons as managers. She was broken up at Kaohsiung in 1980.

Glenlyon 1962 11,918 543.8x74.7x43.5 — 7,022 20 knots
B Nederlandsche Dok & Sch Mij., Amsterdam.
Built for the Glen Line and transferred to the China Mutual Steam Navigation Company in 1975 and Ben Line management in 1977. Laid up at Tilbury in 1978 and purchased by Univan Ship Management of Singapore, becoming *Emerald Express*, operating for Tabard Shipping Company of Monrovia. She was broken up at Kaohsiung in 1979.

Flintshire 1962 11,926 543.8x.74.7x43.5 — 7,007 20 knots
B Van der Giessen Schps, Krimpen.
Built for the Glen Line and transferred to NSM 'Oceaan' in 1974 and Elder Dempster Line in 1977, on charter to the Nigerian National Line. She undertook charters the following year and was laid up at Singapore, where she was purchased by Univan Ship Management. Renamed *Orient Express* for Bastion Maritime Incorporated of Monrovia. She arrived at Kaohsiung on 11 May 1979 to be broken up.

Aeneas 1972 15,498 182.6x22.4x14.2 metres Diesel 11,227 15½ knots
B Astilleros Espanoles SA, Saville.
Built for Cunard Brocklebank Bulkers as Cunard Carrier and purchased by Silverdale Company Limited, becoming *Aeneas* in 1978. Sold to Caroline Maritime (Pte) Limited of Singapore and to Transocean Maritime Agencies. Renamed *Leros Endeavour* in 1987, owned by Dayak Corporation, Piraeus, and *Eli Marie* in 1989 by Gaard Shipping A/S. She became *Norbel Bulk* in 1995, and on 1 April, she arrived at Malta with a cracked hull and did not leave until repairs were completed later that year. She was sent to Keelung, where she was laid up and was auctioned and sold at Shanghai Maritime Court, becoming *Sunny Bulk*. She was never actually owned by Ocean Fleets but was managed and manned by them.

RS Ixion 1977 4,627 113.5x17.6x9.0 metres — 2,859 20 knots
B Kurushima Dock Company, Imbari.
She was built as *RS One* for Glass Container Lines of Liberia and chartered by the Blue Funnel Line for the service between Ellesmere Port and Jeddah in 1977-79.

RS Jason 1977 4,633 113.5x17.6x9.0 metres — 2,859 20 knots
B Kurushima Dock Company, Imbari.
Built for World Patent Corporation and chartered to Ocean Fleets in 1977-79. Ocean Transport & Trading contribution to Overseas Containers Limited.

Cardigan Bay 1972 58,889 290x32 metres — — 23 knots
B Howaldtswerke-Deutsche Werft AG, Hamburg.
Transferred to P&O Nedlloyd Container Line in 1998, becoming *Marion 2* in 1999. She arrived at Alang on 2 March 1999 to be broken up.

Flinders Bay 1969 26,756 227x31 metres — — 21½ knots
B Howaldtswerke-Deutsche Werft AG, Hamburg
She arrived at Alang on 31 October 1996 to be broken up. Work commenced on 10 March the following year.

Kowloon Bay 1972 58,889 290x32 metres — — 23 knots
B Howaldtswerke-Deutsche Werft AG, Hamburg.
She was re-engined in October 1981 and sold to Chase Manhattan Limited and leased back to Overseas Containers Limited. At 2.15 on 24 November 1989, she went aground 30 miles north-east of Sumatra, Indonesia, causing major damage to her bow. She was refloated four days later and towed to Singapore to be repaired. Renamed *NOL Delphi* in 1996, *P&O Nedlloyd Texas* in 1997 and *Texas* in 2000. She arrived at Shanghai on 22 September 2000 to be broken up.

Liverpool Bay 1972 58,889 290x32 metres — — 23 knots
B Howaldtswerke-Deutsche Werft AG, Hamburg.
Renamed *NOL Risso* on charter to Neptune Orient Line in 1996 and P&O Nedlloyd Liverpool in 1998. She was broken up at Panyu, where she arrived on 14 October 1998.

Tokyo Bay 1972 58,889 290x32 metres — — 23 knots
B Howaldtswerke-Deutsche Werft AG, Hamburg.
Renamed *NOL Steno* in 1996 on charter to Neptune Ocean Lines and *P&O Nedlloyd Tokyo* and *Jay Matadi* in 1998. A fire started in her engine-room on 24 August 1998 in position 15.53N 112.50E on passage from Hong Kong to Alang in ballast. The crew of fourteen were taken off by *P&O Nedlloyd Barcelona*. The fire was extinguished and she was taken in tow by the tugs *Taikoo* and *Salvage Queen* to Singapore for repairs to be completed. She arrived at Alang to be broken up on 9 October that year.

Kaduna. (Malcolm Cranfield Collection)

Dixcove. (Malcolm Cranfield Collection)

Several Elder Dempster vessels were transferred to the ownership of the Ocean or China Mutual Steam Navigation Company, including the following:

Eboe 1952 9,378 154.8x19.6x9.6 metres — — 16 knots
Registered under the China Mutual Steam Navigation Company in 1974 with the Blue Funnel Line as managers.

Dixcove. (Malcolm Cranfield Collection)

Ebani 1952 9,396 154.8x19.6x9.6 metres — — 16 knots
Managed by the Blue Funnel Line and owned by the China Mutual Steam Navigation Company in 1974.

Kaduna 1956 5,599 138.7x18.0x9.5 metres — — 15 knots
Transferred to the China Mutual Steam Navigation Company in 1972.

Dixcove 1959 5,905 140.2x19.0x8.2 metres — — 14 knots
Transferred to the China Mutual Steam Navigation Company and back to Elder Dempster ownership in 1972.

Forcades 1963 7,689 141.5x19.0x7.6 metres — — 16 knots
Transferred to the China Mutual Steam Navigation Company and back to Elder Dempster ownership in 1973.

Pegu 1961 5,764 141.9x18.0x8.0 metres — — 14 knots
Transferred to the China Mutual Steam Navigation Company and back to Elder Dempster in 1972.

Pegu.

ALSO AVAILABLE FROM AMBERLEY PUBLISHING

Cunard *A Photographic History*
Janette McCutcheon

ISBN: 978 1 84868 064 7
£19.99

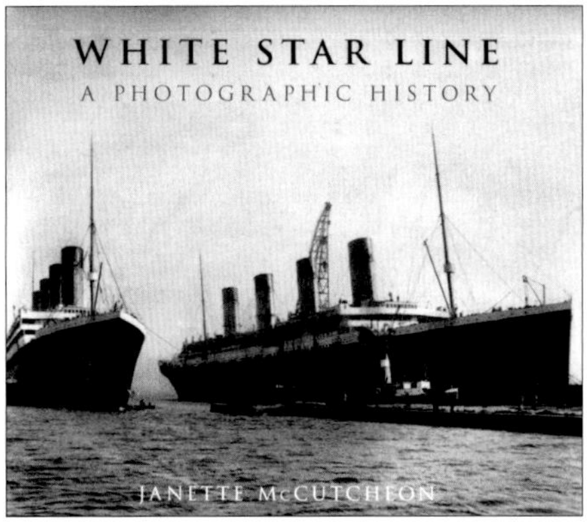

White Star Line *A Photographic History*
Janette McCutcheon

ISBN: 978 1 84868 054 8
£19.99

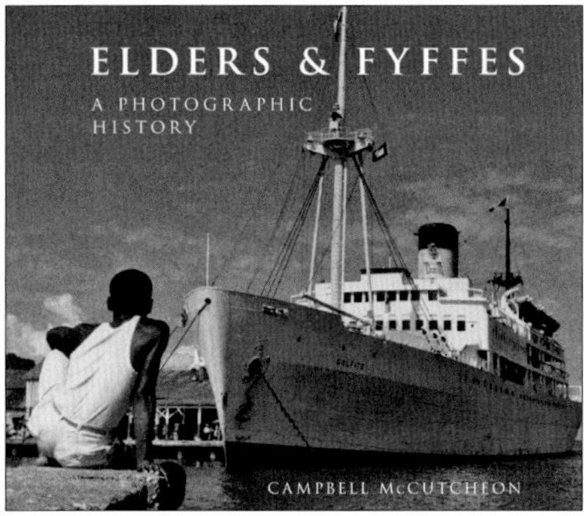

Elders & Fyffes
Campbell McCutcheon

ISBN: 978 1 84868 060 9
£19.99

RMS Queen Mary *Transatlanic Masterpiece*
Janette McCutcheon

ISBN: 978 1 84868 056 2
£19.99

RMS Queen Elizabeth 2 *The Last Great Liner*
Janette McCutcheon

ISBN: 978 1 84868 055 5
£19.99

Ships of the Mersey
Ian Collard

ISBN: 978 1 84868 058 6
£12.99